AF292359

THE BOOK OF MAGICAL LIVING

8 SECRETS TO INNER POWER

POPPY JAMIE

———— * ————

"We are not limited by circumstance, just by
our belief system. When you think bigger, dream
limitlessly and challenge old patterns, you can
literally rewire your brain to believe in possibility –
with incredible outcomes. You have to dare to
dream it, dare to believe it and dare to do it. I
attribute my business success to quantum thinking
and a limitless mindset and I know this book will help
others discover the magic of that mentality too."
– CHARLOTTE TILBURY MBE, PRESIDENT,
CHAIRMAN, CHIEF CREATIVE OFFICER AND
FOUNDER OF CHARLOTTE TILBURY BEAUTY

"A beautiful reminder of life's quiet wonder and the
healing, nurturing power of nature. This book is
a soothing tonic for our modern world."
– CAROLE BAMFORD, ENTREPRENEUR
AND FOUNDER OF DAYLESFORD ORGANIC
AND BAMFORD

"I got goosebumps reading Poppy's book – her
words connect to the deep, intuitive wisdom
inside us, awakening something within.
Truly healing, and... magical."
– LILY JAMES, ACTRESS

———— * ————

Published in 2026 by New River Books
Unit 105, Leroy House, 436 Essex Road, London N1 3QP
www.newriverbooks.co.uk

1 3 5 7 9 10 8 6 4 2

A CIP catalogue record for this book is available from the British Library.

ISBN: 978-1-915780-35-5

Printed and Bound in the UK using 100% Renewable Electricity at CPI
Group (UK) Ltd, Croydon, CR0 4YY.

Illustrations: Esther Palmer

This FSC© label means that materials used for the product have
been responsibly sourced.

To my wise witches.
My mother, Pippa Jamie, and also
to Ruth Nahmias and Deike Begg –
thank you for teaching me
how to live a magical life.

"Magic is a way of living."

– Carl Jung

———— * ————

You'll notice the pages of this book are
numbered backwards.
This is because the road to living with magic
is a journey back to the wisdom already within you.
Magic feels like falling down the rabbit hole
and seeing life with new eyes.
You begin to question what "normal"
really means, to remember that the invisible
shapes the visible and that the deepest truths
are the ones logic cannot explain.
You start to notice signs, synchronicities and
whispers of insight, arriving from nowhere and
everywhere at once. Ideas appear. Intuition sharpens.
New science is now validating ancient mysteries.
If you're ready to create magic, influence the realm
of energy, and live a life filled with wonder, read on.

———— * ————

Contents

Prologue:
Welcome to the world of magic

"It's in our cells, DNA, blood, and bone. Human memories for millennia were based in a magical world. If we follow the path of magic, it takes us on a voyage into the older, wilder, more primitive parts of the brain, into the hidden depths of the unconscious, highways and byways of the spirit; into the realms of human imagination."

– Vivienne Crawley, *Wild Once*[1]

A coincidence too perfect to be chance.
A knowing that arrives before the facts.
It doesn't make sense, yet you've felt it too.

Deep down, there's a part of you that believes in magic because, just occasionally, it can come tumbling into your life unannounced. Suddenly, you're face-to-face with the person you're destined to fall in love with. A life-changing opportunity knocks. Or you look back and realise the blessing in *not* having got what you thought you wanted.

Too often, you've been taught to doubt what you can't explain. To ignore gut feelings. To trust logic.

However, somewhere in your core, you know:

Something far more mystical is happening.

The universe communicates in a language you once knew,
but have forgotten how to see.
It's time to remember that language.

You are about to learn eight ancient secrets that
unlock inner power,
make life move in your favour,
expand intuition,
draw strength from nature,
and tune you into *energy*.
Good fortune begins in the unseen.
Magic is the art of working in harmony with natural forces.
It is the bridge between who you are and who you're here
to become.

The rabbit hole awaits

The power of this book is hard to fully express. Over the years
it's been written, I've lost two late-stage pregnancies. On each
occasion, baby names were whispered and plans excitedly
made. And then, in a single moment, everything changed.
Like water slipping through hands, dreams dissolved.

As I struggled with the ache of loss, this book became
potent medicine. Through the shadows of grief and confusion, timeless wisdom revealed a different way to see life.

What you are about to uncover is not new. It's the echo
of tales as old as time, a weaving together of philosophies,
cultural anthropology, oral traditions and teachings of many
spiritualities and schools of thought.

We often touch the mystical most easily at life's edges, in
moments of birth or death. But nurturing that connection
daily allows every stage of life to become more meaningful.

When life is falling apart, magic reminds you that fortune can change, that *you* can influence how life unfolds. And when things are going beautifully? You need magic just as much to expand, to evolve, to stay in flow.

So if you're navigating unexpected change, feeling uninspired, or just ready for better fortune, I hope these pages offer you what writing them gave to me – a way to fall back in love with life.

What is magic?

The oldest word we have for magic is *heka*, coined in Egypt more than four thousand years ago. First inscribed inside Old Kingdom royal tombs, it is among the earliest writings in the world, older than religion and science.[2] Heka refers to divine creative energy, the pulse that flows through every person. From the birth of a human to the conception of an idea, it names the crossing from possibility into existence.

The Greeks later gave us the word *magic*, inspired by the Persian magi – wise men devoted to ritual and cosmic understanding. But it was through the Hermetic texts, which fused Egyptian wisdom with Greek philosophy, that magic evolved into a deliberate practice. Magic became not just a matter of luck, but a sacred discipline of internal transformation, in alignment with unseen forces – a means of creating change.[3]

As the centuries passed, the wisdom magic gave people became feared. It was branded dangerous, condemned as heresy, and systematically hidden (especially from women). Those in authority did everything they could to suppress it – it wasn't helpful for ordinary folk to be empowered. By the 20th century, magic risked vanishing altogether, until mystics such as Dion Fortune, a trained psychoanalyst, fought to reclaim it.[4] She described magic as "the art and science of causing changes in consciousness at will."[5] In other words, magic is a form of spiritual physics – the inner power to shape reality through energy. Far from being mysterious or "dark", Dion believed magic was a skill that belonged to everyone.[6]

Most of us have felt magic without calling it that. Have you ever noticed how your emotions alter time? When you're anxious, minutes crawl. When you're happy, hours fly. Your state of being bends what you experience. Modern science echos the ancient knowing of *Anima Mundi*, Latin to describe the 'World Soul'. First articulated by Plato, it describes how everything shares a single living intelligence. We are made up of the very elements of stars and galaxies: 93 per cent of the human body is stardust.[7] If what surrounds us also lives within us, then one must inevitably affect the other. A card trick may entertain through illusion, but real magic stirs something far deeper. It opens a mysterious channel between you and the world around you, where healing, synchronicity, good fortune, and your wildest dreams can take form.

The science of magic

Magic and science have long been pitted against each other – one dismissed as fantasy, the other crowned as fact – as if they were mutually exclusive. But look closer, and their boundaries begin to blur.

Magic has always been tomorrow's science. The success of science lies in its repeatability. Once a phenomenon becomes reliable, it is no longer called magic. Imagine the first time someone made a cake. How magical it must have been to see how a few ingredients could create something entirely different. To someone in 1800, an aeroplane would

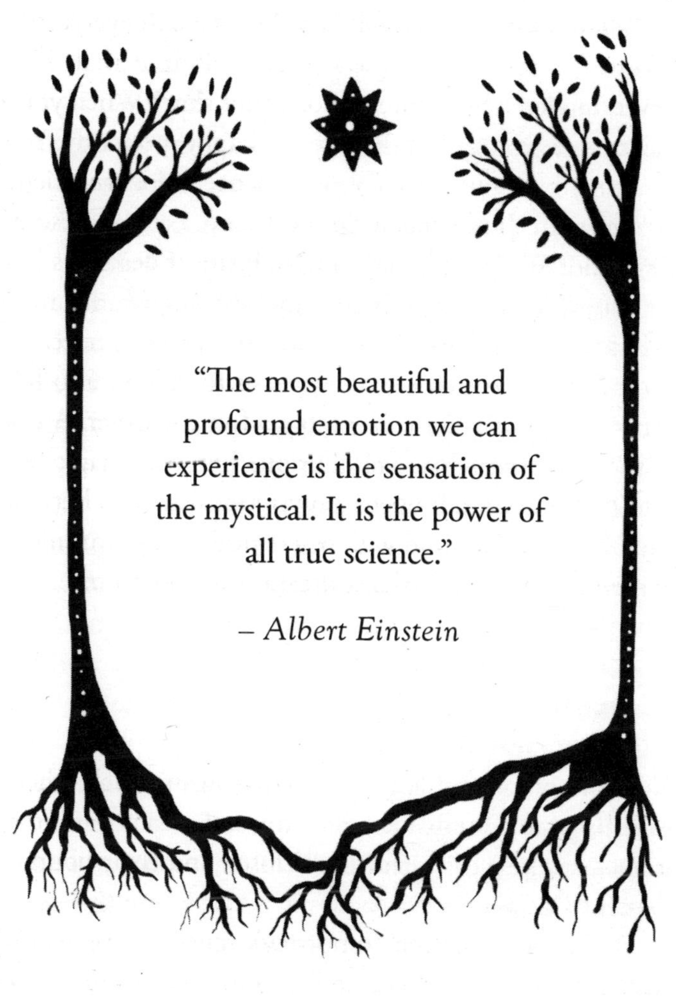

"The most beautiful and
profound emotion we can
experience is the sensation of
the mystical. It is the power of
all true science."

– Albert Einstein

have looked like sorcery. A combine harvester, a monster. To speak of "energy fields" would have sounded delusional. But quantum biology now reveals that the body is electric: every thought, heartbeat and breath generates currents of energy, and wherever there is electricity, there is also a magnetic field. The same is true of the Moon. Once dismissed as astrological fluff, modern chronobiology confirms that lunar rhythms influence our biology. Emergency rooms grow busier during full moons, birth rates subtly rise, plants and animals shift their behaviour. If the Moon can move oceans, why wouldn't it stir us too? We are, after all, made mostly of water.

In nature, what first appears "random" often turns out to be a hidden order. Think of the weather or the flocking of birds, at first glance they seem unpredictable, yet each follows patterns and laws so intricate and complex, we can't always trace them. Coincidence works in much the same way. Is it just random to bump into the person you were just thinking about miles away from home? Or was there a message hidden in this encounter? When we dismiss meaningful moments simply because we don't understand them, we risk more than overlooking insight. We reject an invitation to a world far greater and more mysterious than we can imagine – a world of magic and meaning.

Take the placebo effect: belief alone can trigger measurable healing, comparable to medication. Simply thinking a treatment will help can alter our chemistry, mood, and health outcomes.[8] But what is placebo if not magic by another name; clear evidence that invisible forces within create visible outer results? I was once told about a doctor who gave his patient a pill to help her get pregnant after years of trying unsuccessfully. The miraculous happened. She got pregnant. On her next visit to the doctor, she asked how the pill had done this. "It did nothing," he replied. "I gave you the taste of what it feels like to believe in the future." She had been taking a sugar pill all along. The mind can be the greatest magic wand.

Even quantum physics now confirms what ancient mystics already observed: there's a force that connects everything. At the subatomic level, nothing stands alone. Objects – and we ourselves – are vibrating fields of energy, deeply intertwined. Science has now proven that the simple act of observation can alter the way a particle behaves. It seems implausible that attention alone could influence how life unfolds, and yet it does. Logic tells us that separation should mean disconnection. But in 2022, the Nobel Prize in Physics went to scientists who proved otherwise: once linked, particles can remain bound across time and space, moving as if still one. Perhaps this is why we sometimes feel another's thoughts from miles away or sense someone just before they call.[9]

The more we discover, the more we realise how little we actually know. Even NASA admits we have mapped only 5 per cent of the universe; the remaining 95 per cent is a mystery.[10] We've built rockets, split atoms, edited genes, yet we have barely scratched the surface. The unknown is not a void to fear, or something to be shut down. It is the very soil of possibility. Any great scientist knows that the absence of evidence is not evidence of absence. This is why we must keep an open mind, for it is in mystery that groundbreaking discoveries, and magic itself, reside.

A miracle can happen at any moment, and that's what makes life enchanting. Just consider the odds of your existence; science estimates the chance of being born is roughly 1 in 400 trillion. And yet, here you are. And of all the books in all the moments, you're reading this now. Is that random, or something perfectly orchestrated to reveal an important message? A friend recently gave birth earlier than expected. Hours after her baby arrived, she realised it was the exact day her father had died two years before. No longer was that day to be one of sadness; it had become one of joy. "Just a strange coincidence", some might say, or was it a sign that those we love are still looking after us, even when they're no longer physically here?

Magic asks the questions science cannot yet answer.

The Great Forgetting

Our ancestors lived in constant dialogue with the mysteries of life, listening to dreams, reading signs in nature, and trusting instinct as a compass. They understood that the visible and invisible are woven together in sacred ways we can feel but not always explain.

But then came the Age of Reason, when science turned into the new religion and our ability to hold space for the unknown began to fade. Proof replaced prayer. Logic replaced wonder. Intuition was dismissed as unintelligent. And though we gained knowledge, we lost a more primal kind of knowing.

When we stopped valuing what can't be measured, the Great Forgetting began, and we're still suffering its consequences. For example, in 1968 NASA designed a creativity test to identify people who could think differently, notice what others overlook, and connect ideas in unexpected ways. When this test was given to 1,600 children, the results were startling: at age five, 98 per cent scored at the "genius level" of creativity. By age ten, only 30 per cent did. By fifteen, just 12 per cent. And among adults, that number dropped to just two.[11] The data reveals a sad truth: as we grow up and become conditioned to swap imagination for instruction and intuition for approval, we unlearn the very gifts that once made us brilliant.

Children remind us what we need to reclaim and resee as special. A four-year-old can notice ten times more details than the average grown-up.[12] They still see the beauty and difference in the ordinary. Where we see a forest, they notice the trees' personalities. Where we see the sky, they find shapes in the clouds. As our sensitivity to subtle details fades, so too does our ability to notice valuable insights. Experiments show that six-year-olds can spot a fake smile faster than most adults, which begs the question: what are you overlooking because you're seeing only what you expect – or want – to see?

The Great Forgetting hasn't just changed how we understand the world; it quietly rewrote who we believed we had to be. The rise of technology has numbed these senses even further. As we become more dependent on systems and software, we risk abandoning our oldest human superpower – intuition. AI can rearrange what already exists, and find answers to known phenomena quickly, but it cannot dream, create from silence, or feel another's presence.

This new paradigm is failing us. Nearly one in two people face mental health struggles,[13] a clear sign of a culture that has forgotten how to nourish the human spirit. We're encouraged to value life's riches in money, power and hierarchy, while neglecting life's true gold: a radiant life-force energy, community, nature and a peace of mind. As psychologist Sharon Blackie writes, "We can possess all the fine goods that our civilisation has to offer us; we can have important jobs, and social status ... but without a sense of belonging to the world, we feel empty and our lives lack meaning."[14]

But what has been lost can be found. Our imagination, intuition and creativity are ancient technologies that can be rewilded. They guided humanity long before algorithms, and they still hold the keys to what comes next.

My journey

Although I didn't recognise it at the time, my life began close to magic. My mother is a healer, and she taught us to treasure the small details. While other children might have visited Disneyland, she made sitting in the pouring rain on a Devon beach, eating soggy cucumber sandwiches, just as fun. With her healing hands and positive reinforcement, situations somehow always unfolded better than anticipated, from broken bones recovering quicker than doctors expected, to sniffles suddenly vanishing. But like many others, as school, work and heartbreak pressed in, that connection dimmed, and I fell prey to the Age of Reason's matrix. Doubt and insecurity filled the gap where openness and optimism once lived. From my personal life to my career, everything began to feel off track. I lost sense of who I was or where I wanted to go. I slipped into the trap of comparison, believing everyone else had it better.

So, I turned to science. Science, I was convinced, with its analytical methodologies, would have the answers to my anxiety and stress. I dedicated ten years to studying psychology and neuroscience, creating a technology platform to support digital therapy. I began tracking everything from my sleep to my steps. And yet, despite all this studying, all my schedules and spreadsheets, I never quite found what I was looking for. Understanding how the brain works is undeniably helpful, but knowing the roles of the amygdala, prefrontal cortex or hippocampus can't take away the pain of rejection and disappointment or the confusion of feeling lost. Textbook science, for all its brilliance, falls desperately short in matters of the heart and soul.

Life began to change only when I found my way back to noticing magic. Along that journey, I found people who rekindled my forgotten dreams and sparked hope where darkness had settled. These people shared stories revealing ancient lores of how the universe worked that gave me goosebumps. They described life as a game of snakes and ladders, the snakes as necessary lessons, the ladders as unexpected gifts, both valuable in equal measure. They healed my wounds, awakened my desires and predicted life-changing events. But most importantly, they reconnected me with the cosmic powers that shape life.

You might know some of these people already. They live beyond the matrix – untethered from trends, unphased by opinion, radiant in self-acceptance and guided by their instinct. They move through life with quiet reverence for its beauty, its grief, its mystery. Not because it is easy, but because they embrace *amor fati* – the love of what is. For them, every experience is sacred and designed for their evolution. They transform the bad, celebrate the good. They are alchemists. They are free. They are powerful.

They are witches.

What makes a witch? The truth behind the myths

The word *witch* is provocative. It might conjure images of cauldrons, pointy hats, and broomsticks. But a true witch is far from the caricatures that pop culture has stereotyped and parts of religion have demonised. Some scholars link the word to the Proto-Indo-European root *weik* meaning "to bend" or "to twist". Others, to the Old English *wicce* and *wicca* associated with knowledge, awareness and understanding. Both interpretations resonate. To be a witch is to have an inner power: the skill to work in harmony with unseen forces and, in doing so, bend circumstances and fate. Witches are

"I think that all
women are witches,
in the sense that a witch
is a magical being."

– *Yoko Ono*

practitioners of magic, or as Dr Vivianne Crowley defines, "The witch is a worker of energies."[15]

Here's the irony. When men like Albert Einstein worked with the invisible, they were called visionaries. Einstein's theory of relativity was inspired by a teenage dream chasing a beam of light. But when women explored the mysterious, they were branded dangerous.

In truth, witches were never evil spell-casters boiling frogs in shadowy forests. More accurately, they were our earliest herbalists, healers, pharmacologists and midwives. They were people who believed in the human ability to create change. But as religion became a tool for political power, the persecution of the "witch" evolved into a strategic method of control.[16]

Throughout history, the witch archetype conveniently resurfaces at moments of instability – during economic collapse, recurring plagues, or famine. When systems fail, blame needs somewhere to land. It is therefore unsurprising that the most violent witch hunts of the late sixteenth century were following political conflict and social upheaval. Older women were among the first to be targeted, particularly those who had inherited property or wealth. Homes were taken. Money was seized. Yet the most significant theft was quieter and more insidious: the dismantling of entire lineages of feminine wisdom. It became risky, even deadly, to think for oneself, and we are still living with the consequences.[17]

The accused had likely never even spoken an incantation but the oppression worked. Individuals became scared of their inner power and ancient traditions were driven underground. Clearly, magic and those who practised it were never the true threat. The threat lay in what magic represented: a life shaped from within.

The truth is, "witch" is not a gender or a fantasy; it is

someone who practises magical wisdom. Slowly but surely, prejudice is changing. We are at a critical moment; when science is now validating what was persecuted. Is a spell not simply the sort of goal-setting practice, meditation or ritual that psychologists now encourage? Is a potion not just a blend of nature's gifts, like a herbal tea to soothe or a remedy to heal? Penicillin, discovered by Alexander Fleming in 1928, is perhaps the most excellent potion of all. The mould *Penicillium notatum* comes naturally from fungi. And isn't prayer just another path of intentional magic? A mental act intended to work with a divine source to influence the world in some way.

German philosopher, Arthur Schopenhauer, once said, "All truth passes through three stages. First, it is ridiculed. Second, it is violently opposed. Third, it is accepted as being self-evident"; or as Ghandi similarly wrote, "First they ignore you, then they laugh at you, then they fight you, then you win." The witches and their wisdom are finally winning, ironically with science as an unexpected ally.

As a way through my grief – as I searched for inspiration and a renewed childlike joy for life – the image of the witch kept returning. Psychiatrist Carl Jung once wrote that when the soul is ready for transformation, it speaks to you through recurring symbols. Eventually, I couldn't ignore the call any longer – and began interviewing as many magical women and men as I could find. From all different faiths and backgrounds and of all different ages; my body tingled as I listened.

The magical secrets you are about to discover can transform your life. They are more than just a quick wave of the wand; they offer a discipline. Before we begin, there are two truths that underpin everything.

First, the law of assumption, or confirmation bias as psychologists call it: life unfolds according to your deepest expectations. As you believe, so you experience. The magical realm, abundant with possibility, welcomes all explorers, but it remains hidden from those who do not seek it. As Roald Dahl reminds us, "Those who don't believe in magic will never find it."

Second, the law of cause and effect, or causality as it is known in physics. The universe longs for equilibrium, so whatever you give inevitably returns. You hold far more influence over what you receive from life when you tend carefully to what you send.

To be a witch is to live in harmony with these natural laws. In doing so, you develop an inner power so profound that luck and fortune are no longer accidents, but responses. You may already be a witch, or perhaps you live next door to one. But the most thrilling part is this: everyone has the potential to activate magic.

Welcome to your magical life.

"Where science leaves off,
divine magic begins."

– *Phyllis Curott*

————— * —————

Each magical secret in this book
is paired with a tarot card.
These archetypal symbols act as mirrors,
or gentle prompts, to prepare your inner
world for what's to come.

————— * —————

When the Wheel of Fortune appears, it's a reminder that there are greater patterns at play; moments that seem random often carry deeper meaning and can unexpectedly change our lives. When we are aligned with what we truly want, the wheel turns in our favour, and the right forward path opens up.

The universe is speaking, learn to read the signs

"The world is full of magic things, patiently waiting for our senses to grow sharper."

– W.B. Yeats

Mystics have long understood the power of signs and symbols as guides. Swiss psychologist Carl Jung formalised this idea, coining the term "synchronicity" to describe those inexplicable moments linked not by cause, but by meaning.

A coincidence is a random collision of events, like wearing the same yellow t-shirt as someone else on your morning train. Synchronicity is something far more profound, where something other than the probability of chance is involved.[18] In other words, it is a kind of divine choreography revealing a message. Moments of synchronicity may signal an important event ahead, offer gentle reassurance that "all shall be well", or serve as cosmic encouragement to make a decision. Perhaps a friend gifts you a book that holds an answer you desperately need, or you notice an advert for your dream job as you wait for a delayed bus. Synchronicities are never random, they are invitations to pay attention. They urge you to look deeper. When you know these signs could be around any corner, every day holds the potential for revelation.

In her book, *Synchronicity*, my favourite author and Jungian expert Deike Begg writes, "Synchronistic events frequently intervene to warn us if we are on the wrong path. If we persist with dogmatic determination in going our own way and disregard signs to the contrary, we will sooner or later have to pay for our foolishness … I have found again and again that when we are on the right path, when what we are doing is what we are meant to be doing, doors open, opportunities present themselves, and progress becomes relatively easy."[19]

Noticing the universe's nudges is one thing, but deciphering their meaning is another. Synchronicities don't always arrive neatly gift-wrapped with a bow. In fact, at first glance, you might want to send them straight back to the universe. Interpreting signs takes practice, and sometimes the meaning behind a sign becomes clear only much later.

My first dramatic encounter of this came a few days before finishing school. I was walking into my very last exam, ready to taste freedom. I could see the finish line and all the exciting plans waiting for me on the other side. I'd worked obsessively for this moment – colour-coded notes, mind maps in scented pens, revision timetables plotted to the minute. I knew precisely which university I was going to, and nothing could derail me.

The English Literature paper was perfect. All my favourite questions were there; I wrote for pages and finished with time to spare. My heart fluttered – this was the moment all those late nights had been for. And then a phone rang.

Who would bring a phone into an exam when we'd all been warned we'd be disqualified? I thought. I glanced around, confused as to why the boy next to me was not moving to turn it off. Then reality hit. It was coming from … my pocket.

It couldn't be. I *always* left my phone at home during exams. It was *always* on silent. But there it was – my pink flip phone, buzzing loudly in my jacket. I fumbled to hand it to the invigilator, my face redder than red, eyes wide as dinner plates. One unexpected call, one mistake, and my life as I knew it was over.

I was disqualified and subsequently rejected from university. While everyone else celebrated the start of their lives, I was forced to return to school and re-do it all. I couldn't understand how something so small could have dramatically changed my life so much. Surely, this couldn't be just a terrible coincidence …

On reflection years later, I realised I'd been sent many warning signs leading up to this point. My acceptance letters had been strangely lost in the post, resulting in countless calls to the university to confirm if I really was accepted. The train was even cancelled on my trip to visit the campus. What I couldn't see then was that all these synchronicities were divine messages. My determination had made me blind to the signs that this plan wasn't right for me, and eventually the universe was forced to step in dramatically. An unexpected phone call during an exam, from someone who had never called me before, rerouted my destiny. I had to create a new plan. I got a job, moved to London, stumbled into a career that I ended up adoring, met my best friends, and built a life more magical than I could ever have imagined. What "mistakes" or "rejections" have actually propelled you forward?

Divine clues

My mother understood synchronicity long before I ever read Jung's words. Whenever she felt deeply worried, a white

"Signs can transform us.
Signs can take us from one state
of being to another. They can take
us from despair to hope, from
lost to secure, from stuck to soaring."

– *Laura Lynne Jackson*

feather would appear out of nowhere, as if to comfort her. One Christmas Day, during our annual pre-turkey walk, we spotted a pristine white feather in the middle of a muddy field – untouched by the weather. My mother pointed it out, smiling. "Poppy, look!" It was unusual. There were no birds in sight, yet there it was, impossibly clean, as if placed there just for her. My grandmother had passed away when my mother was turning 30. Ever since, she has believed these synchronistic moments – seeing white feathers – are her mother's way of sending a message from beyond.

However they appear, synchronicities serve as important guideposts along our journeys, pointing us towards our true purpose and desires. My mum visualised her mother sending signs; for you, it might be a friend, a favourite pet, a god, or the universe. How we interpret these signs depends on our sensitivity to calls from a realm beyond our physical senses. I often notice a heart shape in unexpected places: in leaves or trees, at the bottom of coffee cups or in clouds. Whenever a heart reveals itself, it reminds me that I am being cared for.

My long-term Kabbalah* teacher and astrologer, Ruth Nahmias, once compared synchronistic events to finding a £5 note on the floor – one person notices it while 99 others are too distracted to see it. "Don't be the one to let meaningful moments pass by without noting their significance; there is no such thing as a coincidence, just coordinated instances", she would remind me. Making a conscious effort to notice patterns turns your daily experiences into a magical

---

* Kabbalah is an ancient practice that explores the deeper workings of the universe and the nature of life. On a literal level, the word *kabbalah* means "receiving", so by studying the philosophy, one is receiving wisdom. Just as Buddhism offers a philosophy rooted in Indian traditions and Hindu theology, Kabbalah is a mystical philosophy rooted in the Jewish lineage – a map for understanding creation, consciousness and the soul's journey.

dialogue. "Why is this happening to me?" becomes "What am I supposed to learn from this?" I am deeply reassured by this idea, as it helps me remember that we are never travelling our path without a universal force guiding us.

Coincidence or fate?

My second life-changing synchronicity happened a year after the phone intervention – and this time it was a more obvious sign. I was travelling to a small town in the English countryside with my university housemate, James. Nursing hangovers, we woke up late and, after rushing to the station, we missed our train. We boarded the next available one and collapsed into our seats, sharing a table with a stranger. James struck up a conversation with our table companion, and within seconds, I noticed her American accent. It felt unusual to meet an American travelling in such a remote part of the countryside. And I was interested: just the night before, I had been planning my first-ever trip to Los Angeles. Lo and behold, it turned out that our new friend was from Los Angeles too. My heart raced. With Ruth's lessons on synchronicity fresh in my mind, I wondered: could this moment be a magical intervention? There was only one way to find out. "You're from California? No way!" I exclaimed. "I'm going to LA in a few weeks!"

She replied, smiling, "Really. Why are you going?"

"Because I'm a TV presenter," I said, trying to hide my nerves, given I'd only technically presented three shows (two minutes long) at the time, "and I really want to move there one day."

Then the unbelievable happened. "You're a presenter? I work with MTV." I was hyperventilating inside. Here I was, in a place I'd never been, face-to-face with someone connected to my dream network employer and future home, and all because I'd missed my intended train. Or had I? The universe was winking at me.

This kind stranger went on to make some introductions that catapulted my move to America, got me my first job, and opened the next chapter of my life. That morning, everything had seemed to be going wrong, but in actuality, a missed train was about to light up the path ahead. A perfect example of synchronicity and a reminder to think twice about life's frustrations. A divine intervention might just be occurring.

Jung believed synchronicities happen when our inner world and the outer world momentarily align, when what we feel inside is echoed by what unfolds around us. It's as if life answers a question you are consciously, or unconsciously, asking. Curious about how such coincidences could happen, he sought answers from a Nobel Prize-winning physicist who noticed a similar mystery in the quantum world. In physics, certain particles remain connected – when one moves, the other instantly responds – even when separated by vast distances. To Jung, this resembled what he saw in human experience: events and emotions seeming to "move together" across time and space[20] – further proof that everything in the universe, from thought to matter, dream to event, is woven together by an invisible thread.

Synchronicities can't be repeated and so it's easy to dismiss them. But if you practise pressing pause on your rational need to explain everything, you create space for a deeper consciousness to emerge. I once asked Google's former CEO and leading scientist, Eric Schmidt, what he thought about concepts like synchronicity, destiny and the human soul, to see how someone so data-driven viewed these arguably "fluffy" phenomena. He replied, "I'm a scientist, so I don't *know* about things unless we can prove them.

But we don't fully understand how biology works. We can't even make a complete digital version of the human cell yet. There are mysteries in life. I think the most important ones are consciousness and souls. My guess is that we will never fully understand them. That is magic to me." Even if we cherish science and data-led understanding, like Eric, we can all hold space for mystery. Being curious to the universe in this way will only welcome in more wonder and most importantly, hope. Albert Einstein famously said, "There are only two ways to live our lives; one is as though nothing is a miracle, and the other is as though everything is a miracle."

Numbers as signs

"The world is full of magic things, patiently waiting for our senses to grow sharper," wrote Yeats,[21] and numbers are among the most persistent of those things. A clock lands on 11:11, a receipt totals £22.22, a hotel door echoes your birthday. Like a little tug, a moment can be marked as significant.

Across history, numbers have been treated not only as tools for counting but as carriers of essence. The Greek philosopher Pythagoras, regarded as the father of Western numerology, taught that the physical world was made of numerical vibrations and that all things resonate with a specific number. From this ancient tradition grew the belief that certain numbers hold special power and even fortune.

Repeating sequences are often referred to as *angel numbers*. As the name suggests, certain numbers act like divine messages. Sometimes the message is immediate, sometimes it ripens with time but if you notice a certain number following you around, see it as an invitation to look deeper.

Angel numbers decoded

Sequence	Invitation	Mystical Roots
111 (11:11)	A doorway to new beginnings and alignment. Pause and name what you want to call in.	In Pythagorean numerology, 1 is unity, creation, the spark of all things. It carries the energy of beginnings, individuality, and divine will. When repeated, it signals alignment between mind and universe, a master number moment when intention begins to manifest.
222	Balance and trust. A reminder to soften overthinking and re-centre.	The number 2 has long represented duality and partnership (moon cycles, sacred feminine, yin/yang). Mystics saw it as a sign that opposites seek harmony rather than conflict.
333	Creativity and play. A nudge to lighten up and go deeper into purpose.	The triad was sacred to Egyptians, Greeks and Christians alike. From the triple goddess to the Holy Trinity, it symbolises creativity and spiritual growth through joy.
444	Integrity and foundations. Build steadily; trust the work you're doing.	In Kabbalah, 4 reflects stability and manifestation (the four worlds, the four elements). To see it in repetition is a reminder to turn higher vision into practical action.
555	Change is unfolding. Trust transition and lean into the unknown.	The number 5 speaks of change. It's the moment when life begins to move again, when stability turns into growth. In Taoist philosophy, the five elements (wood, fire, earth, metal, water) are a living cycle, each transforming into the next. In Tarot, it's the shake-up that brings renewal. And as an angel number, five signals that change is not chaos, but guidance; a divine nudge towards freedom.

Sequence	Invitation	Mystical Roots
666	Rethink balance between material and spiritual. Realignment is needed.	In sacred geometry, 6 represents harmony and balance – the hexagon found in honeycombs, crystals and snowflakes. It's the pattern where spirit meets matter. The number six reminds you to find equilibrium in your life, particularly between your professional and personal responsibilities and between giving and receiving energy. 666 invites you to re-focus on spiritual growth instead of material concerns.
777	Spiritual awakening. A sign you are supported and guided.	Across traditions, 7 is the number of mysticism and completion, the seven heavens, seven chakras, seven days of creation. Repeated, it affirms divine alignment.
888	Abundance and flow. A reminder that energy circulates.	8 evokes infinity and eternal cycles. In Chinese traditions it is the number of prosperity, abundance and financial success. In Hermetic thought it signals balance between spiritual and material wealth. When you see this number, see it as a confirmation that abundance (in any form) is on the way.
999	Completion and release. Time to surrender what no longer serves.	9 closes the cycle, the final number before renewal. In mystical systems it symbolises wisdom, endings, and readiness for transformation.
13	Sacred transformation. Rebirth. Divine feminine, magic and manifestation.	13 has long been misunderstood as unlucky. In ancient traditions, it symbolised the divine feminine and the natural cycles of renewal – 13 moons in a year, 13 months in the pre-Roman lunar calendar. To the Egyptians, it was the sacred number of Isis, goddess of magic and rebirth. In Kabbalah, 13 signifies "echad", the oneness between human and God. Only later, when the feminine was devalued and scripture misread, did 13 fall from grace. In truth, it remains a number of renewal, transformation and manifestation.

Working with numbers

Numbers are not only observed; they can be partnered with. Many of the world's most creative and successful figures have tapped into the power of numbers and woven them into their lives and legacies. Coco Chanel believed fervently in the luck of five. Her legendary Chanel No. 5 was launched on the fifth day of the fifth month, chosen from the fifth sample presented. She even scheduled her fashion shows for the fifth of each month. Christian Dior favoured eight, founding his fashion house on October 8th, 1946, and naming one of his early collections *En Huit* ("In Eight"). Taylor Swift is famously devoted to 13: born on the 13th, she turned 13 on Friday the 13th, her first album went gold in 13 weeks, and since then she has tucked the number into track lists (with 13-second intros) and performances, and has even sat on the 13th row at award shows

If you are interested in finding a number to work with, a simple way to start is your Life Path number, drawn from your date of birth. Add the numbers from your birth date together – the day, the month and the year. Keep adding the digits of the new number until you get a single digit. For example, someone born on 2nd March 1989 would add 2 + 3 + 1989 to make 1994, then 1 + 9 + 9 + 4 to make 23, then 2+3 = 5. Some traditions hold 11, 22 and 33 as "master numbers", and therefore wouldn't reduce them to a single digit. These master units represent an extra-special energy.

Making things happen

Scientists and mystics agree that we have a limited capacity to see and understand everything. Just as we can't see ultraviolet light, gravity or Earth's magnetic field, we may not fully understand why certain synchronicities happen because we simply can't see the full picture. The person you "randomly" meet tomorrow could be the one who saves your life in 20 years' time or introduces you to the love of your life. With this recognition of our limited perspective, life takes on a more sacred flow. We may never know for sure why things happen in the moment, but two things are certain: one day it will make sense, and nothing is accidental.

That said, while some forces remain beyond our understanding, others are quietly shaped by us. The famous double-slit experiment, first performed in 1801 by Thomas Young at the Royal Institution, revealed something fascinating (and challenged all existing ideas): particles behave differently when you look at them. Light and matter can act both as waves and as tiny particles – a cornerstone of quantum mechanics. When no one is watching, they move like waves, passing through both slits at once and creating a striped pattern. But the moment scientists set up instruments to track which slit particles are passing through, the striped wave pattern vanishes, and the particles behave like solid balls instead.

Why does this matter? Because it demonstrates a profound truth: observation changes how reality appears. Where we place our awareness alters what happens. This is not just a quirk of subatomic particles – it's mirrored in life itself. Biologist Rupert Sheldrake's research on "the sense of being stared at" has shown that many people can detect when they are being watched, as if human attention itself has weight and influence.[22] Just as particles shift when observed, so do we. You are not merely witnessing life; you are shaping it with every thought and act of attention.

Take watching a magic trick, for instance. When a performer gestures to the right while making the real move

"The path that is uniquely ours is our own responsibility to find and follow. We cannot blame our parents, partners, society or God for preventing us from treading it. Unless we stop blaming, we have no chance at all to begin living our own precious lives."

– *Deike Begg*

on the left, we're captivated by the illusion. Has the coin truly vanished, or has our focus simply been redirected?

The same principle applies to real life. We experience what we choose to focus on. If we live as the audience, we'll be pulled by every headline, distraction and fear. But if we choose to live as the magician – consciously deciding where to place our attention – we start to influence what happens.

When we feel stuck, confused or unhappy, it's easy to assume our environment is the cause of our problems. We blame it on the fact we hate our job, or we're in the wrong relationship. But being magical is knowing change starts from within. Ancient societies knew this. If a hunter couldn't find food, he didn't blame the forest, he visited the village shaman. Both knew there was of course plenty of food out there; the problem wasn't scarcity, but the hunter's inability to see opportunities in front of him. A shift in awareness was needed, not a new environment.

Hundreds of years later, the same principle still applies. It's easy to believe there are no good jobs, no aligned partners, no open doors. But statistically, that simply isn't true. The question isn't whether opportunity exists. It's whether we're tuned in enough to see it.

The science behind being luckier

To an outside observer, magical living can resemble luck, but science explains why some people notice signs and act on opportunities, and others don't. Professor Richard Wiseman studied over 1,000 volunteers for nearly ten years to understand why some people are luckier than others.[23] He had a hunch that lucky individuals, like magical folk, tend to have a more optimistic outlook and view chance encounters and unexpected events as fortuitous. Their openness and positivity incentivises their brains to spot possibilities that others might miss.

Magician Derren Brown demonstrated something similar in a TV experiment.[24] He found a man who considered himself "unlucky" and practically intervened to make his life objectively "lucky". He planted winning lottery tickets on his doorstep, set up interviews that would have rewarded him with cash had he answered the questions, and even left money on the floor right in front of him. Despite these "lucky" set-ups, the man missed every opportunity. He didn't bother to scratch the lottery ticket, didn't stay long enough to be interviewed, and walked straight past the cash on the floor. Despite being surrounded by luck, he couldn't see it. So, what explains this difference in awareness?

It turns out our brain is constantly filtering reality based on existing assumptions. According to information theory, the human body sends around 11 million bits of information per second to the brain, but the conscious mind can process only about 50 bits per second. That means we're aware of just 0.02 per cent of the information we receive. The rest is edited out before we even realise it. Just think about how much is lost in the 99.98 per cent of information we unknowingly filter out.

The part of the brain responsible for this filtering process is called the Reticular Activating System (RAS). Your RAS decides what information gets through based on what feels familiar or important to you; your past experiences, traumas, beliefs and desires. It acts like a personal assistant to your brain, screening calls before they reach the boss.

Just like a social-media algorithm, your RAS shows you more of what you've already expressed interest in. For example, if you assume the world is unsafe, it will confirm this by spotlighting every story that proves that belief. If you assume good opportunities don't exist, your RAS will quietly ignore the ones that do. Thinking about buying a red car? Red cars become relevant, and your RAS will begin to point out every red car you pass.

Here's the vital part: you can consciously retrain your RAS. As the magical lore says, "Life unfolds according to your assumptions." If you believe signs and synchronicities will guide your path, and fortune is waiting to be revealed, your RAS will start showing it.

Take my mother, who believes she's endlessly lucky despite all the grief she's had to manage in her life. She will often call me just to say, "I am so lucky. I just spotted a blue tit in the garden" or "I found a parking space just outside the supermarket." From the outside, it seems like luck. But perhaps, she's just trained herself to notice life's tiny gifts. They say money makes more money. I'd say: luck makes more luck and magic makes more magic.

How do you train your RAS to spot more magic?

It's no coincidence that nearly every sacred text, across cultures and faiths, teaches that gratitude opens the door to abundance. As author Rhonda Byrne reminds us, prophets and teachers throughout history have echoed the same message: Muhammad taught that giving thanks safeguards future blessings; Buddha spoke of having no reason for anything but joy and gratitude; Lao Tzu said that contentment makes the whole world yours; Krishna accepted every offering with joy; King David gave thanks for all creation; and Jesus expressed gratitude before performing each miracle.[25]

Counting your blessings is one of the oldest, simplest and

most powerful ways to invite more magic into your life. The more you consciously notice and appreciate the good things, the more you train your mind to do so automatically. No matter who you are nor where you are in your life, everyone benefits from this practice. The art of gratitude helps open communication pathways, priming your inner mechanics to look outwards and proactively notice the good things instead of being consumed by what's going on within.

Each morning, I develop my magical practice by writing a gratitude list[26] and repeating these simple affirmations:

I expect the unexpected.
Life only gets better.

The universe is always trying to communicate with you. This might appear as numbers, words or symbols. Regardless of the language in which the message comes, learn its vocabulary. When you do, the path forward lights up with winks. The cosmos has a great sense of humour, so don't forget to have fun.

The High Priestess asks you to trust your greatest gift; your intuition. She holds a scroll marked TORA, a symbol of hidden knowledge. With the Moon at her feet, she reminds you that wisdom is often concealed from sight. She stands at the threshold between the seen and unseen, inviting you to pause, be still and tune in.

Unlock intuition
and reawaken your sixth sense

"Logic works well with a known and finite set of facts, but when we make life choices, we are operating against the background of the unknown future. Trusting our intuition, which operates outside everyday time and space, becomes the most rational course of action."

– Dr Vivianne Crowley[27]

Magic has always been closely entwined with intuition. But in a world increasingly shaped by technology and artificial intelligence, our overwhelmed minds have stopped thinking for themselves. We've begun outsourcing our decisions, our direction, and even our desires to external sources: algorithms, influencers, experts and screens. We rarely ask, "What does my intuition say?" It's easier to follow the crowd. But the trouble is, the crowd is lost too.

This is what drew me to witches, sages and wise ones. Figures who, for centuries, held a sacred place in communities. They are the ones we turn to when our own sense of direction falters. These people aren't paralysed by indecision or distracted by chasing validation. Their hearts and minds are in quiet harmony, led not by logic but by a deep, unwavering trust in their intuitive guidance.

One cold February afternoon, a distant friend messaged me: "Do you want to visit an intuitive guide? She gives readings for charity at a local pub." Not that this friend knew, but I'd had a terrible couple of weeks. This felt like a synchronicity – an invitation from the universe – and it was precisely what I needed. I sat down with an elderly woman, hoping she might help me gain some clarity around the work issues I'd been navigating. "What would be most helpful to discuss today?" she said. I responded that a general life reading would be helpful, with a focus on work.

Within a few minutes, she paused, looked at me, and said, "I keep hearing the word abortion." Does that make any sense to you?" I froze. It had been just two weeks since I'd devastatingly lost a baby at four-and-a-half months pregnant. Due to severe complications, I'd had to undergo a surgical procedure. I was still overwhelmed by grief and confusion. But how did she know?!

"Yes," I said in disbelief. "I've just had one."

She nodded. "Ah. That makes sense now. Don't worry, he's coming back."

Again, I was floored. "He's coming?" How did she know I was supposed to be having a boy?

She asked if I had any questions. I had a million. But I chose one: "Why didn't he want to come to Earth?"

She looked at me gently. "He wants to come back at a better time, for both of you."

I was speechless. But then something shifted. A wave of deep knowing washed over me. In my bones, I felt the truth of it. He was coming back. And just like that, the confusion and heartbreak began to soften. In its place: a quiet, steady sense of acceptance, and hope.

Here's the secret: we all hold that same intuitive power. The role of the witch, the mystic, the guide isn't reserved for the chosen few. It lives within all of us; the ability to know about things that logic can't explain.

It's scary how quickly our data-obsessed world has over-ridden this gift. Everything is measured, from sleep scores to follower counts, as if numbers alone can define how well we're living, more than our own intuitive knowing. But how useful is it, really, to wake up and be told you slept badly? You might be stepping into the most magical day of your life, so why begin it by relying on what an algorithm says? We're not machines. We don't switch on and off with a tap of a button. What makes us innately magical is our sixth sense, the quiet wisdom that detects what isn't said, sees what isn't shown, and feels truth before it's proven.

In a *Harvard Business Review* study, 85 per cent of CEOs said intuition was critical to their decision-making.[28] Jeff Bezos once noted, "All of my best decisions in business and in life have been made with heart, intuition and guts – not analysis." Despite being recognised by business legends, intuition is still second-guessed and regarded as inferior to other data points.

When I sat down with intuitive reader Kathryn Schiff, she described intuition as "the part of us that's tuned in to what's happening around us – even the things we can't see in this 3D world. As energetic beings, we're constantly communicating with energy. Intuition is how we understand that language. Think of a time you felt an undeniable pull towards a deci-sion – a tingling, a deep yes in your body that you couldn't explain. That's your intuition speaking. Intuition is the skill to notice details that are mostly overlooked. Research has observed that only 7 per cent of communication is verbal.

The other 93 per cent is conveyed through body language, tone and energetic presence. Neuroscience proves we register emotional and nonverbal cues up to a third of a second faster than logical conscious thought.[29] This is why we must remember to trust our feelings because our body often knows the truth long before our mind can make sense of it. Intuition is a superior intelligence available to us that we've forgotten how to nurture.

Visionaries who trusted the unseen

Steve Jobs created the trillion-dollar Apple empire based on intuition. He famously said: "Have the courage to follow your heart and intuition. They somehow already know what you truly want to become." His deep meditation practice helped him see a future no one else could imagine. When everyone said consumers wanted more features and more buttons, Jobs did the opposite. He stripped everything down to a screen in its simplest form. Experts said it would fail, but Jobs trusted his gut and it changed the way we use technology forever.

Isaac Newton is known as one of the greatest scientists for discovering the laws of gravity. But he wrote over one million words on alchemy – far more than he did on physics. Even the economist John Maynard Keynes noted that Newton was "the last of the magicians." His breakthroughs came from believing in something beyond the physical senses – he valued the unseen world even more than the visible one.

Charlotte Tilbury knew she was building a global beauty empire long before there was proof. "I would be backstage at fashion shows, doing make-up on supermodels, knowing I was going to create something much, much bigger," she told me once. Charlotte didn't have a business plan yet or data, only a deep, cosmic trust. Eight years later, that vision became a billion-dollar brand.

It's not just entrepreneurs and business leaders who channel intuition; artists, musicians and all creatives access a deeper inner knowing to bring their visions to life. The act of taking an idea from the depths of the subconscious and manifesting it into the physical world is what the Ancient Egyptians observed with *heka* – the divine energy of creation and the birthright of every human. The people who change the world aren't necessarily the most logical or sensible, but they are the most connected to their intuitive compass. This is the foundation for magic.

The source of our tingly knowing

Some argue that intuition is just the brain recognising patterns faster than we can consciously process. Yet research shows young children, who are not strong at pattern matching, score higher on intuition. Their brains are better at noticing tiny details. Children often have a favourite chair because of one microscopic detail, even though to an adult, the chair looks identical to others. This is what drives an intuitive sixth sense – an ability to feel and notice exceptions.

Some mystics and philosophers understand intuition as a more divine process: a delicate transfer of information from a greater intelligence. Roberto Assagioli, a pioneer of spiritual psychology, called intuition a bridge, a link between our everyday mind and the greater field of wisdom shared by all (a collective conscious).

I imagine intuition to be like tuning in to an invisible radio, ideas floating in the atmosphere, waiting for the right receiver. You can see this in action when people across the

OUR COLLECTIVE CONSCIOUS

globe, without ever speaking, arrive at the same thought at the same time.

For example, Charles Darwin and Alfred Russel Wallace both outlined the theory of evolution around the same time, and yet they lived at opposite ends of the world, when it was difficult for information to travel. CRISPR gene editing was discovered in parallel by two unconnected labs. Pop culture often reflects the same phenomena when two films or novels, eerily alike, are released within weeks of each other. Just a coincidence? Or evidence for a shared pool of ideas.

Perhaps ideas aren't invented, but channelled. Not owned but remembered. Not random, but perfectly timed.

Why can't we always hear it?

Over a century ago, German philosopher Hermann Keyserling observed, "Only intuitive people are free. And it's for this reason that only they are our great discoverers, pioneers, and innovators."[30] He also warned that when intuition erodes, we risk losing the very thing that drives human progress: the ability to imagine, innovate, fuel creativity, and cultivate trust in ourselves. Sadly, in today's world constant distraction, social media and propaganda are stripping us of independent thought and inner knowing. The convictions of others can easily drown out intuition if we're not careful. As children, our instincts are sharper because we haven't yet absorbed the biases that blur our purest truth. A child might instinctively recoil from someone who feels wrong, while an adult, trained to be polite, overrides that inner signal. To reconnect, we must first unlearn, or as Dion Fortune writes, "Let us have the courage of our convictions and follow our own deeper promptings."

Herbalist Terri Conroy explained to me how modern life has made intuition harder to access: "I think modern life closes people down. Even electricity has interrupted things. As soon as people had televisions, they began focusing on them, and their ability to see the supernatural was greatly reduced, as their minds became closed off to it. But in Ireland, especially where I live, we didn't get electricity until the 70s. We have been living with the seasons for much longer. When daylight fell, we used candlelight. And if you ask my generation or older, everyone I know will have had some kind of unusual, inexplicable experience. I remember asking a friend about her psychic ability, and she said she stopped seeing things once electricity arrived. With the advent of the Industrial Revolution and technology, the side of the brain open to detail and the mystical quickly turned off."

Our intuition hasn't disappeared, but the world has become so overwhelming that we forget we even have it. All is not lost; we can unblock our cosmic reception. One of the easiest ways to begin is by stepping into unfamiliar places to break the patterns of daily life and avoid falling into auto-pilot mode. By simply taking a new route to work, your brain is forced to sharpen its ability to notice things.

The intuitive body

It's often easier to start connecting with intuition through the body rather than the mind. For some, intuition might show up like a magnetic pull or an undeniable gut instinct. For others, it manifests as a tightness in the chest, a sudden headache, or an inexplicable wave of exhaustion. I have many friends who say their vagina is their intuitive tool: when something isn't right, a UTI will take hold. My stomach

"Pay very close attention to your
body because it doesn't know how to
lie to you, and pay very little attention
to your mind because it is lying to
you all the time."

– The Witches Circle

is mine. Whenever I ignore my intuition, my stomach rings the bell.

I once stayed in a relationship that wasn't right, but the idea of ending it filled me with so much anxiety that I pushed my instincts aside. My partner had been planning to take me on a romantic getaway, but on the day we set off, my stomach erupted in excruciating pain. I spent the entire trip in agony. Looking back, my body was clearly trying to tell me what my mind wasn't ready to accept: I was on the wrong path. Which part of your body feels "sensitive"? Perhaps this is your intuition trying to convey a message.

Like a muscle, intuition grows stronger with use. To act on it can feel scary at first because sometimes, you will get it wrong, and that's ok. It takes time to recognise the difference between a "yes" and a "no". Lean in to small messages and test them out. A wonderful mystic taught me this simple exercise to help. Close your eyes while placing one hand on your heart and one on your stomach. Think of something you know is a BIG yes, such as a person you love or a place that brings you joy. Notice how the feeling sits in your body. Do the same for an obvious no, something that feels deeply wrong or misaligned. Now, think of something you're unsure about, a decision you're weighing up. How does it make you feel? Observe whether the sensations match the yes or the no. Practise this with small decisions, even everyday ones. Do I want eggs or porridge for breakfast? Do I *really* want to go to that dinner on Thursday? The more you do it, the stronger connection you will build.

Our in-built North Star

One of the challenges in reconnecting with your intuition

is learning to separate true intuitive knowing from anxious interruption. Mystical teacher Dr Kate Tomas once told me, "Intuition is calm. Anxiety, however, is stressful – often triggered by external sources or memories." This distinction is essential. Intuition is information, not emotion. It arrives as a quiet knowing, a sense that simply is, rather than a spiralling thought loop. You might experience an emotional reaction to an intuitive thought. For example, intuitively you feel a potential date or person is not quite right for you, but subsequently fly into a panic about being alone, which just muddles the original knowing. When you develop awareness of where intuition ends and emotion begins, you can start to trust this inner voice. At first, this means testing it in small ways, leaning in to the gentle prompts, seeing where they lead, before making bigger decisions with confidence. Unlike logic, intuition doesn't deal in simple black-and-white answers. No person or situation is wholly right or wrong. Life is complex, and intuition can help you navigate the endless grey areas with mystical clarity.

A few years ago, I was facing a pivotal decision about a job opportunity. After rationally weighing up the pros and cons, I decided to say yes as it would be financially beneficial. Still, I felt a nagging uncertainty, a knot of anxiety in my stomach. Then, a quiet inner voice urged me to reconsider. This was my intuition speaking. I declined the offer, but once I'd taken the leap – my mind erupted with "what ifs". What if I had made the wrong choice? What if I regretted it? What if this jeopardised my financial security? Thanks to Dr Kate's guidance, I recognised this second wave of anxiety for what it was: not intuition itself, but my emotional reaction to what my intuition had told me. Watch out for this common experience: a gut feeling followed by a surge of doubt and fear.

Premonition: leaning into whispers of the future

While intuition helps us sense what lies beneath the surface of a situation we're already facing, premonition takes things a step further, offering glimpses of the future beyond the linear confines of time.

Few things feel more magical than having a stranger see into your future with astonishing accuracy. There may be no adequate scientific explanation for how this is done – just evidence of how little we truly understand, and how beautifully mysterious our universe remains. Extrasensory perception begs the question: do time and space behave the way we think they do? If someone can glimpse the future … has it already happened?

Some mystics believe these moments come from what French philosopher Henry Corbin called *the imaginal realm* – a space between worlds. Corbin drew on Persian mystical traditions, which described this as a subtle dimension that sits between the physical and the spiritual, a realm where meaning is received rather than invented.[31]

This isn't the same as imagination. The imaginary is something we consciously create, like picturing a unicorn in a teacup. The imaginal, by contrast, feels as though it arrives from beyond us – through a dream, a vision, a symbol, or an image that carries significance we couldn't have deliberately constructed. These glimpses, whether they appear through dreams, intuition, or synchronicity, can feel like flashes of insight. For me, the recurring symbol of the witch felt imaginal in nature: it didn't immediately make sense, yet it carried weight, acting as a sign that invited deeper exploration.

In January 2020, under tremendous stress from work and feeling uncertain about where I should live, I decided to visit a psychic in Ojai, California, with my best friend. This psychic was as disconnected as you could be from the modern world; he had no internet and could be contacted only via landline. A friend had used his services for years and swore by his accuracy, so I sent a cheque through the post to book my appointment.

The psychic used playing cards and astrological birth charts drawn by hand to tap into the imaginal realm for future insight. As soon as I entered his office, he told me, "I see you at home. You need to go back home to England. Spend time with your parents and do nothing for six months." I was floored. With a company to run, travelling every week and in the middle of a fundraise, the idea of doing nothing for half a year seemed absurd. I argued, "But I have a company that helps people's mental health. I can't just stop." He laughed and said, "No one can ever really help someone else's mental health; that requires the person to help themselves." This was hard to hear, and instantly I decided this psychic witch must be wrong. Do nothing for six months? That was just not an option.

I left his house disgruntled, dismissing his advice and writing him off as a fraud (of which there are many in this area of work and we must always operate with discernment regarding information we're told). I vowed never to return. Eight weeks later, the COVID pandemic hit, and I flew home to live with my parents. My company received an offer to sell, and the world came to a standstill. I was forced to stop. Suddenly his farfetched vision made complete sense. While I sat in the English countryside for the first time in 17 years – for months on end – I had a deep feeling that everything was unfolding exactly as it should.

Mother Shipton's special powers

Great fortune tellers have always been revered members of communities, and their premonitions continue to astound us. Mother Shipton, known as The Great Prophetess of England, began life in a cave in Knaresborough Woodland in 1488. She became a renowned herbalist and she married a carpenter. Her prophecies started with localised events before extending to the passing of kings and the Great Fire of London. Despite her cunning practices, she avoided persecution for witchcraft, likely owing to the accuracy of her predictions, which made her a valuable resource to those in power. Here is an extract from a prophetic poem she wrote in 1562, predicting a future full of cars, the internet, cruise liners, and the changing role of women, among many other eerily on-point observations:

> … Carriages without horses shall go
> And accidents fill the world with woe
> Around the world, thoughts shall fly
> In the twinkling of an eye:
> Water shall yet more wonders do,
> Through lands man shall ride,
> And no horse nor ass be at his side:
> Under water, man shall walk,
> Shall ride, shall sleep, shall talk:
> In the air, man shall be seen,
> In white, in black and green:
> Iron in the water shall float
> As easy as a wooden boat:
> Then tax and blood and cruel war
> Shall come to every humble door
> The women shall adopt a craze

And cut off all their locks of hair
To dress like men and trousers wear
They'll ride astride with brazen brow
As witches do on broomsticks now …

Her predictions are, for the most part, uncannily accurate. Similarly, Nostradamus, the 16th-century French philosopher and folk healer, continues to fascinate with his book of prophecies, *Les Prophéties*. Many claim his cryptic verses predicted events as diverse as the French Revolution, the rise of Hitler, and even the attacks of September 11th 2001. Another mystic who made several predictions before her passing in 1996 was Baba Vanga of Bulgaria, who predicted the rise of AI, stating that non-human intelligence would become commonplace.

Animal instincts

Animals provide even stronger evidence for the universal existence of such sixth-sense skills and access to a different realm of information. They demonstrate a strangely accurate ability to predict natural disasters. Before the 1997 Assisi earthquake, peculiar animal behaviour preceded the catastrophe: rats swarmed restaurants, and dogs howled incessantly. On another occasion, in the 1970s, the Chinese government successfully evacuated cities before earthquakes based on nothing more than reports of unusual animal activity. Long before the 2004 tsunami, elephants, monkeys and birds abandoned coastal areas in Sri Lanka, India and Indonesia, seemingly sensing the impending disaster. Such incidents happened so many hours in advance that they can't wholly be written off as mere reactions to distant sounds or rumblings.

Biologist Rupert Sheldrake has dedicated many years to studying premonition within animals. One of his experiments involved investigating dogs that seemed to know when their owners were returning home, even from miles away. Sheldrake studied a dog named Jaytee, who consistently went to the window shortly before his owner returned, regardless of the mode of transport used or the randomness of her arrival times.[32] This isn't a unique phenomenon; he found that 52 per cent of dog owners observe this behaviour too.[33, 34]

The science behind premonition

Rupert Sheldrake has also conducted fascinating research on humans. In one study, he found that 45 per cent of people have had premonitions, particularly with telepathic telephone calls, where someone seems to know who is calling before answering.[35] Following the September 11th disaster, he initiated an investigation into precognitive dreams, and received over 75 reports from New Yorkers who experienced dreams about the attacks leading up to them.[36] Many dreamers reported visions of planes crashing, burning skyscrapers, and clouds of dust rolling through the streets. Some shared their concerns with friends or family before the event happened, lending credibility to their experiences. A few individuals chose not to go to work as a consequence, which ultimately saved their lives.

A few years ago, I personally witnessed how mysterious a premonition can be. I was going through one of those heartbreaks that completely flattens you. I had been crying for a solid 24 hours and felt confused and terrified about the future. Then, out of the blue, I received a message from Ambi, a woman who had taught me meditation a decade earlier but now lived halfway across the world. Ambi and I hadn't spoken in over a year.

October 31st, 6:16pm – Ambi
"Poppy! You were in my dream last night. Just wanted to check in. Hope all is well. Lots of love xxx"
My heart stopped.
6:17pm – Me
"Ambi, I can't believe this. I was in hysterics all night. Just went through a break-up."
6:17pm – Ambi
"Oh Poppy. I knew something was wrong, you came to me in the dream asking for help. We're always connected, even in silence. The message I received for you was clear: trust in love. What you want already exists, just not in this moment. You will have the family and relationship you are looking for."

Despite the comfort her words brought me, my scientific mind couldn't help but question the timing of Ambi reaching out. How could someone feel my despair from across the world, in a dream? This felt like clear evidence of an imaginal realm beyond time and space.

Quantum science is beginning to provide some possible answers. In the 1930s, physicist Erwin Schrödinger described a mysterious phenomenon he called "entanglement" – the discovery that two particles can remain connected even when separated by vast distances of space and time.[37] Touch one, and the other somehow feels it. Was Ambi's message a human version of this?

For decades, even within scientific circles, the idea of particles "communicating" across vast distances and time was considered fringe. Many scientific journals refused to publish research on the topic, and academics were warned against pursuing it. Physicist Sandu Popescu admitted his adviser warned him against a PhD in the field, saying, "Look, if you do that, you will have fun for five years, and then you will be jobless".[38] But, despite criticism and scepticism, finally, in 2022, the Nobel Prize in Physics was awarded to the scientists[39] who proved the existence of quantum entanglement through ground-breaking experiments. Their work revealed that particles could in fact remain entangled no matter the distance, defying the conventional understanding of physics. Entanglement begins to sound a lot like what mystics have always described: that the universe is not a collection of separate parts, but a single, interwoven field.

From this perspective, phenomena like telepathy or premonition aren't supernatural at all, but natural extensions of our interconnected biology. Just as birds navigate using invisible magnetic fields, the emotional and energetic bonds between people may create subtle fields of connection, allowing information to travel through resonance rather than physical signals. In this view, consciousness isn't locked inside the brain, it moves through shared fields of mind and feeling, linking us across distance, species and even time.[40]

Divination: a tool to develop intuition and premonition

Divination is one of the most popular forms of common magic. The word comes from the Latin *divinatio*, derived from *divinus*, meaning "of the gods" or "inspired by the divine". In Western esoteric traditions, there are various types, including tarot, astrology and geomancy, and divination by earth, otherwise known as dowsing. Ancient cultures used various

"The future is unconsciously
prepared long in advance and
therefore can be guessed
by clairvoyants."

– *Carl Jung*

forms, including oneiromancy (divination through dreams) and ornithomancy (divination through birds and their flight patterns). Julius Caesar, one of Rome's most powerful and influential leaders, consulted diviners throughout his reign, especially for matters of war. His assassination on March 15th was famously foretold by a soothsayer who warned him to "beware the Ides of March".

In all forms of divination, success depends on the diviner's ability to tap into the imaginal realm, beyond their personal biases, beliefs and preferences. It's a sacred art used to reveal wisdom. For the past twenty years, I've turned to tarot readers for guidance. The idea that the cards tell the future can create unnecessary fear, so I like to clarify that divination is a tool for highlighting dispositions rather than fixed destinations; for tendencies and potentialities rather than inevitabilities. The road forward will always present forking paths, and while some forks may feel easier or more familiar, none are beyond our power to choose. Just like the popular Latin motto conveys, *Astra inclined sed non obligat* – "The stars incline us but don't bind us."

Author Benebell Wen of Holistic Tarot explains this well through the example of temptation. If you put me in front of a tray of biscuits, my natural disposition would be to eat one. However, my friend who dislikes sweets won't. Of course, it doesn't mean my fate is sealed, just that my tendencies lean that way. With enough awareness and intention, I can summon the will to choose differently.[41] Fate inclines us, but never locks us in. Or as Deike says, "Character is destiny, but you can change your character."

These days, divination is less about predicting the future than fostering self-inquiry and revealing potential blind spots. In Jungian terms, it helps bring unconscious material to the surface through the power of story and archetypes. That's why many therapists and coaches now use tools like tarot as a creative tool for psychological exploration. Wen explains this nuance: "If I ask you, 'What will happen when I put my hand into the fire?' and you answer, 'You will burn yourself,' are you predicting the future? In one sense, yes. What you're doing is tapping into your conscious knowledge to access information that will provide insight into the most probable outcome of my contemplated action."[42] Divination helps you tap into unconscious knowledge, bring it into conscious awareness, and use that insight to navigate choices with expanded clarity.

The history of tarot

Tarot is a tapestry woven from many cultures. Playing cards first appeared in China during the Tang Dynasty (618–907CE), decorated with mythological references and believed to have been used secretly for divination. Around the same period, Korean shamans reportedly worked with silk pieces arranged into eight symbolic suits, echoing the structure of today's tarot.

Through trade routes, these practices travelled westward, influencing Islamic societies before reaching Europe in the late 1300s, where they evolved into the tarot we know today, passing on knowledge through symbols rather than words. Although the Church often banned cards, tarot seems to have escaped suppression, likely owing to its popularity among the wealthy.

One enduring legend suggests that the 22 Major Arcana were created as a symbolic code to preserve hidden wisdom, possibly linked to the Knights Templar, a medieval Christian military order who were brutally suppressed in the 14th century. It has since evolved into a reliable instrument for spiritual growth. What yoga is to the body, tarot is becoming to the mind – a tool for clarity and connection.

Take the example of my cousin, who had just been offered a temporary job at the company of her dreams. She was thrilled, but it also meant jeopardising her current job, which she liked but didn't love. Unsure whether to take a risk on a temporary opportunity at her ideal company or stick with a safe job she already liked, she asked me to pull cards for her. I closed my eyes, imagining her in my mind's eye. "What should Catherine know if she takes this job?" I pulled a card. The four of wands popped out. Wow. This card is one of celebration. It depicts a joyful scene of two people dancing amidst a profusion of flowers, symbolising the happiness of achieving a milestone. A beautiful wreath, laden with grapes and blossoms, hangs suspended between wands – a tangible representation of success. In the background, a grand castle signifies security. This card is full of happiness and stability; undoubtedly a yes card. It reassured my cousin's personal inklings that taking this new opportunity was a good decision.

Working with the tarot

A standard tarot deck consists of 78 cards divided into two parts: the Major Arcana and the Minor Arcana. The Major Arcana comprises 22 cards that represent long-term psycho-logical and spiritual themes. In many ways, these cards reflect life's journey from innocence, documenting hard lessons and spiritual insights on the path to divine fulfilment. Each card illuminates an aspect of the psyche.

The Minor Arcana contains 56 cards, divided into four suits – Swords, Wands, Cups and Pentacles – which repre-sent more immediate human experiences: daily challenges, relationships, places and the material world.

Swords are associated with the element of air and symbolise intellect, communication, conflict and decision-making. They represent the mind and its processes. Wands are linked to fire and embody creativity, passion, energy and inspiration. They represent the spirit and willpower. Cups are connected to water and symbolise emotions, relationships, intuition and spirituality. They represent the heart and emotional world. Pentacles (or Coins/Rings) are associated with the earth and represent the material world, finances and health.

Tarot is a language of metaphor and there isn't such thing as a "bad card". My friend Pippa says the "Death" card is her favourite because it signals that new opportunities and positive transformation are close by. Sometimes things must fall for something better to rise in its place.

For the past seven years, I've been guided by my gifted tarot teacher, Dieke, whose readings never cease to amaze me. Every few months, I make a pilgrimage to her house as a form of therapy. We talk about life and then turn to the cards. The ritual always feels deeply restorative.

During one visit, I had just been diagnosed with premature ovarian decline, a condition marked by diminished ovarian reserve and an accelerated path towards infertility. The diagnosis was devastating and forced me to face the possibility that I might never become a mother. The anxiety of it all made me book a tarot session to help me come to terms with a reality I didn't want.

During the reading, she paused mid-spread, looked at me intently, and declared, "You are going to be pregnant. Look, this card represents mother and child." I laughed in disbelief, knowing my medical news made that almost impossible. Yet card after card echoed the same message of impending motherhood. I tried to explain the slim chances, but with a

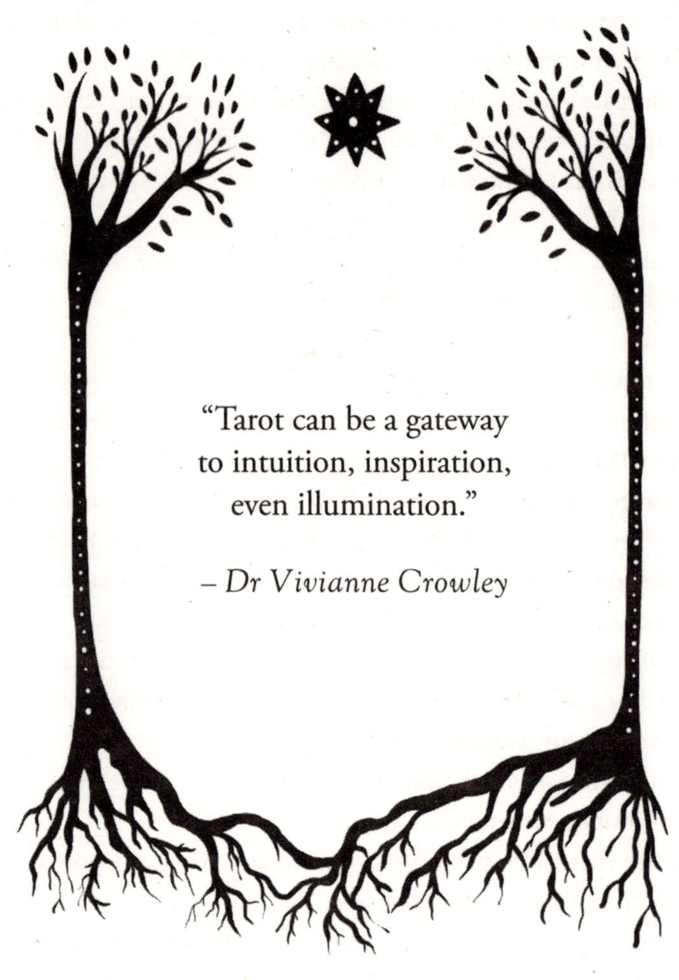

"Tarot can be a gateway
to intuition, inspiration,
even illumination."

– Dr Vivianne Crowley

gentle smile, she said, "I'm simply telling you what the cards are saying. Pregnancy is coming. Call me when you are."

I left thinking the cards probably meant pregnant with a new business or book idea. So, five months later, after a missed period, I reluctantly took a test. I hadn't been planning a child, and with my own biological limitations, along with my partner's fertility being uncertain after cancer treatment, I assumed stress was the reason. To my utter astonishment, it was positive. Against all odds, I was pregnant.

How to draw cards

Like a spider's web, the universe is a vast network of interwoven energies. Every part of it, from the biggest stars to the smallest atom, is linked. When we engage in divination, we're exploring this web, so no card we pull is random. Like synchronicity, there are moments when insight breaks through – brief flashes where something greater seems to speak – and this is what makes life so extraordinarily mystical and magical.

As I've learned to read the cards myself, I've watched my intuition grow stronger. The beauty of tarot is that there are always multiple ways to interpret a card. It's almost like having a conversation with a best friend who points out things you might not be able to see. The combination of the card drawn and the visual imagery prods your intuition to expand awareness. The quality of your answers depends on the quality of your questions. For instance, if you're wondering whether you'll get a job you've applied for, instead of asking a closed question like, "Will I get the job?", it's more beneficial to ask an open-ended question such as, "What can I do to increase my chances of success?" or "What do I need to know about this opportunity?" This invites the cards to reveal layers of insight that would otherwise remain hidden. Perhaps you sense there are hidden tensions, energies or activities that are influencing events, but you want clarity on what they are. Maybe you want to find a better way of achieving your goals. What we should have at the end of a reading is a sense of how to move forward with wisdom and discernment. Over time, I've developed a simple ritual to centre myself before drawing cards. I ask the deck:

> Show me what I need to see.
> Tell me what I need to hear.
> Teach me what I need to learn.

This keeps things open and sets a nice tone to begin.

Swinging between worlds

Just as tarot offers a lens for introspection and guidance, other divination tools, like pendulums, serve as valuable physical extensions of our intuition, allowing us to tune into energetic frequencies and explore our consciousness. Pendulums are a key tool in dowsing, an ancient practice used not only for divine insight but also for locating hidden resources such as water, minerals or even lost objects. Dowsers believe these tools work by sensing subtle energies or vibrations that exist beyond ordinary perception.

The earliest written record of dowsing dates back to the 16th century in German mining villages, where it was likely first used to locate precious metals within the earth. However, there are claims that images resembling dowsing rods have been found carved into Egyptian cave art and appear in other ancient cultures, including Greek, Hindu and Hebrew traditions. Dowsing lost its popularity when people in the church branded it an evil, occult practice, but folk practitioners still needed to find water and other materials underground, so the practice continued in secret. According to Lauren Lingard,[43] this may actually be why a forked stick came to be used for dowsing, as it could be gathered in secret and disposed of after use. Most commonly, a hazel branch would be chosen for its flexibility and long-standing association with wisdom and protection.

As the age of reason and scientific enquiry took over in the 18th century, interest in this divinatory art declined. But not all scientists dismissed dowsing. Albert Einstein is said to have been a practitioner himself, believing that science would one day have an explanation for the mechanism behind dowsing's effectiveness.[44] The fact that today's oil and water companies still use dowsing as an accurate way to inform where drilling should take place demonstrates its lasting value. Several major UK water companies, including Thames Water and Severn Trent Water,[45] have admitted to using dowsing to locate leaks, despite the availability of more modern technologies.

So how does it work? Many believe the pendulum acts as both a receiver and transmitter of unseen forces, translating subtle energies into movement. Think of it like attaching an antenna to your intuition. As soon as earth frequencies are detected, the rods begin to cross, or the pendulum – a simple weight on a chain – starts to swing. Pendulums are thought to respond to your body's energetic field, creating tiny reflexes in your arm and wrist that reveal deeper layers of intuition. When used for personal exploration, diviners ask a question, and the pendulum's movements are believed to reflect answers channelled through the body's own wisdom. Dowsers say everyone has this ability, it's simply a matter of practice, trust and finding the tool that resonates with you.

I once met a venture capitalist who based his work decisions on what his pendulum said. He had previously agreed to invest in my company, but had subsequently pulled out because his pendulum said no. As much as I was bemused that such big decisions could be determined by something so unscientific, in hindsight, his pendulum was right. The company was about to go through some very challenging months. My own mother has a crystal pendulum to which she poses questions and, depending on the answer, the crystal will swing to the left or right. If it doesn't know, it won't move. Her crystal predicted the birth of my brother's baby and the gender. Her crystal also predicted that I'd get back into a relationship with my boyfriend when, at the time, I thought there was no chance of that happening. Perhaps most surprisingly, the crystal revealed I would lose my first pregnancy. When it happened, I found unexpected comfort in rereading her dowsing notes, sent to me five months after she had written down the pendulum's answers. It felt like a gentle reminder that everything was unfolding according to divine order. I'm sure the idea of a crystal swinging sounds on the verge of delusional, but I remain shocked by the mysterious accuracy.

Tips to start strengthening your intuition with a crystal pendulum

1. Begin by holding your pendulum still and asking it to show you a "yes" and a "no" – observe the direction it swings naturally for each.
2. Practise daily by asking simple, low-stakes questions you already know the answer to, building trust in your intuitive response.

3. Ground yourself with deep breaths, stay curious, and treat each session as a conversation with your inner knowing, not a test to pass.

In the end, all these divination tools are extensions of intuition. If we can widen our awareness, we can be guided more fully into alignment with the person we are meant to become. Although we don't fully understand why or how divination works, these magical tools have stood the test of time.

We live in a world that prizes logic, data and certainty, yet beneath that surface hums another kind of intelligence. It's the language of the soul, guiding us when the maps fall short. Whether through dreams, gut feelings, pendulums or cards, the truth is this: the answers you seek are not somewhere out there. They've been inside you all along, waiting for you to listen and remember what you've always known. Phyllis Curott captures this beautifully: "Divining tools are like a lighthouse to a ship at sea, offering guidance in a storm or on a dark and starless night. But the choice of how to alter your course always remains your own."

Temperance teaches that true healing cannot be rushed. She reminds us that life-force energy requires moderation and harmony. The two cups represent opposing forces – the physical and the spiritual, the conscious and the subconscious, the masculine and the feminine. The image signifies the resolution of inner conflicts, leading to peace and wholeness.

Charge your internal power source

"Before a magician can move energies of the universe, they must first master the storms within themselves."

– Israel Regardie[46]

The road to becoming magical requires one essential ingredient: radiant energy. Without it, like a car without fuel, your power to create simply breaks down. Your vibration sets the tone for what's possible. When your life-force energy is strong, the world is alive with opportunity. When it's drained, anxious or scattered, even the simplest tasks turn into battles and magical power is lost.

Mystics and witches have always known what physics confirms: everything is energy. You, me, the chair beneath you, the light in your room are all made of vibrating particles. Magic is the art of directing this current with intention, but of course a strong current is needed first.

Have you ever felt stuck, as if no matter how hard you try, manifestation just won't happen for you? Worse still, everything you try to create doesn't turn out the way you planned? This is not a reflection of your potential. It's a sign that your energy is leaking. A buried emotional wound, lingering exhaustion, or a state of depletion is quite possibly stealing the energy you need to practise magic effectively.

This might sound familiar – because we are experiencing a collective energetic crisis, and it's harming everyone to some degree. Research shows nearly 80 per cent of workers in America feel burned out.[47] No amount of positive thinking can fix exhaustion, it's a louder call for deeper healing.

Think of yourself as a bucket. Emotional wounds, inherited beliefs, misaligned environments, and old stories act as holes that leak precious energy. Despite how much you try to "fill" yourself with success or achievements, those holes make pleasure transient. Good feelings will come and go so quickly that you remain just as empty as when you started. But it doesn't have to be this way. When you begin to address both your inner and outer worlds, you patch the holes and allow the bucket to fill *and stay full*. From that fullness, life-force energy is restored, and you can regain your magical powers.

Just as rivers must flow to nourish the land, your life force must circulate freely to sustain clarity and creation. You'll come to see that magic is far from fantasy, but a practice of psychological wholeness – one rooted in self-discipline, emotional balance, and inner harmony.

The invisible world

The first time I consciously observed the power of energy was just after my 13th birthday, when my father finally agreed for us to get a pet parrot. My mother had wanted one for ages, and after some convincing, T-Pe was welcomed into the family. The parrot – named after my brothers and me – quickly became a source of constant squawking. My mother was the only one who could quieten the bird and would signal him over to land on her finger, then proceed to give him Reiki healing. Reiki is an ancient healing practice that channels universal energy into the body of another living being to promote healing and deep relaxation. Rooted in symbolism and ancient mantras, it is now embraced by millions worldwide, and even hospitals are beginning to integrate Reiki programs. Research found, for example, that patients receiving Reiki after knee replacement surgery experienced significantly less pain.[48]

I witnessed the tangible impacts of this modality firsthand. The moment my mother began her practice, T-Pe would settle, drifting into sleep within seconds. It was mesmerising. Animals can't fake their reactions, so I could see the parrot was responding authentically. My mother's ability to calm his temperament with just energy convinced me that the invisible world is both real and profoundly influenceable. She didn't stop at the parrot; our dogs and even the pet sheep received healing, and they exhibited the same reactions – asleep within moments. From that moment, I wanted to know more. Over a decade later, I trained as a Reiki healer myself and I've been working with energy ever since.

The path to healing

In daily life, we often find ourselves flapping through chaos like T-Pe, agitated and overstimulated. Instead of addressing our emotional wounds, we patch over them with caffeine, alcohol and constant distraction; temporary fixes that push our problems only deeper into the body, leaking us further. Over time, stress becomes addictive. We grow so used to the buzz of anxiety that rest feels unfamiliar, even uncomfortable. Stillness begins to feel unsafe. A dysregulated nervous system doesn't just steal your ability to make magic, it blocks intuition, making you feel even more lost.

For too long, Western medicine has treated symptoms in isolation, overlooking the profound interconnectedness of body, mind and spirit. Did a bad back just appear? Or is it the tip of the iceberg, revealing a deeper story? When you live with magic, a bad back becomes your friend, inviting you on a deeper healing journey to understand the underlying *why*.

Traditional Chinese Medicine, by contrast, has always understood that energy stagnation is at the root of all illness, with practices like acupuncture designed to restore flow. New science is beginning to catch up with research, proving that emotional stress doesn't just fade when an event is over, it can leave lasting imprints in the body. The fascia, a vast web of connective tissue that wraps every muscle, nerve and organ, responds to trauma by tightening and hardening. Over time, this stiffness disrupts the body's healthy circulation, sending constant "alarm signals" to the nervous system.[49] The result is a subtle but chronic fight-or-flight state, quietly fuelling inflammation and draining vitality.

Knowing this, an energy-centred, 360-degree approach to healing becomes essential. If you don't tend to the body, no amount of "mind work" will be enough to make magic effective. The patterns locked in your tissues will continue to drain your life force. As Bessel van der Kolk writes, "Trauma isn't just an event that took place sometime in the past; it's also the imprint left by that experience on the mind, brain, and body."

The vibrations of emotion

Emotions aren't just feelings; they're frequencies. Every mood sends ripples through the nervous system, influencing brainwaves, heart rhythms, and even the electromagnetic field around us. Love and gratitude signal safety to the body, calming the nervous system and creating the conditions for healing and clarity. By contrast, fear, anger and shame activate stress responses that deplete energy, disrupt hormones and cloud perception.[50] True power belongs to the calmest person in the room – the one who can steady their own energy when others cannot.

When we learn that emotions can trigger internal damage, we often label them as "bad" and avoid them. That avoidance doesn't resolve them; it widens the leak. During my interview with trauma expert Dr Gabor Maté, he noted that many cancer patients show a heightened pattern of bitter repressed emotions and resentment. His research builds from a landmark 1974 study that found women with breast cancer were significantly more likely to suppress anger than happier feelings. Suppressing emotions has a correlated risk factor for depression and other poor health outcomes.[51] The research is clear: when you don't fully express what you feel, your body bears the burden.

I experienced the intricate connection between emotional memories and energy during a session with healer Dr Sarah Chiro. As she moved through the energetic field of each organ, she paused and said, "You're holding on to a friendship wound from childhood – a female friendship wound." It landed instantly. My deepest insecurity growing up was the fear of being excluded by other girls. Whether she knew it or not, one school friend seemed to exploit that fear again and again, and I could never say anything. I hadn't realised how much of that pain was still lodged in my body until, during the session, Dr Chiro began to release what had been stored. As the energy shifted, tears came. That old trauma had been quietly draining my life force for years. And now, finally, I could let it go.

An abundant magical life can rarely manifest from someone who hasn't taken the time to release what's been carried in silence. Emotional suppression isn't just a personal habit, it's a cultural inheritance. For centuries, women who expressed rage, grief or desire were branded as unstable, even a threat to society. The "hysterical woman" became a medical diagnosis. Generations of young girls have been taught that "good women" are agreeable and self-sacrificing. Princesses don't shout. Wives don't roar. But what if this centuries-old silencing isn't just limiting, it's making us sick? Maybe the women branded as "hysterical" were revealing something much more profound; intentionally expressing emotions is a route to better health.

Miraculous healing

Our beliefs are so much more powerful than we give them credit for. For example, in a randomised study of systemic inflammation, simply being told that one's treatment is likely to work significantly reduced symptoms, even among people given a fake pill, showing that expectation alone can activate real changes in how the body feels illness and responds to therapy.[52]

The very ritual of taking a pill tricks the brain into believing the body is being supported. In another study, participants given placebo medication for migraines also reported meaningful symptom relief. Such findings prove a simple truth:

"Your biography
becomes your biology."

– Caroline Myss

belief is medicine, and our cells are always listening.[53, 54]

If you can use your mind to send a message to your little toe to wiggle, why can't you send a message of healing? The body can't distinguish between what's vividly imagined and what's physically real. That's why watching a horror film can make your heart race and muscles tense, even though you *know* it's fiction. Your body responds to the signals your mind believes.

My email footer for the past decade has read: "Thoughts become things. Choose the good ones." The placebo effect and the power of imagination prove just how true that is. Be mindful of what you think and say. Your body is always reacting.

Healing all wounds: past and present

My friend Nikki, a wonderful mystic, introduced me to a simple yet powerful framework to address energetic wounds. The emotional needs grid overleaf[55] is designed to provide insights into how past injuries have affected us and how we might heal.

Use this framework to explore and better understand your own needs and where they stem from. Reflect on how emotional wounds show up in your life, then apply these simple actions to gain clarity. As you work through this process, you may start to recognise where your energy is leaking and discover ways to mend and refuel.

Need	Description	Injury	Coping pattern	Magical healing
Attention or validation	A need to be seen, heard and positively reinforced by others.	May feel unwanted, insecure or unworthy.	May behave in ways that are exaggerated or unexpected, fighting to be noticed. May have perfectionist tendencies or a drive to overachieve.	"What can I appreciate about myself?" Write a list of your unique qualities.
Security	A need to feel secure and safe.	May feel abandoned, neglected, uncared for and unable to self-regulate.	May struggle with a need for control, and experience rigidity, hypervigilance, excessive mood swings and withdrawal. May experience clinginess, excessive need for reassurance, or isolation and avoidance.	Life has changed since you first were injured. Write down all the ways you're safer now than you were before. What tools do you have now that you didn't in the past?
Belonging and acceptance	A need to feel accepted, connected and included in a family or group.	May feel left out, lonely, hurt, disconnected and anxious.	May struggle with perfectionism, overachieving, people pleasing; or on the flip side coldness, isolation and avoidance. May experience difficulty in trusting others or take things personally.	No one belongs to everything. Make a list of the people and places that make you feel safe and secure for being exactly who you are.

Coming unstuck

When your life force feels blocked and nothing seems to shift, sometimes you need outside help. I remember a time when I felt completely stuck. For over a year and a half, despite regular meditation and countless hours of therapy, I was caught in a loop of frustration. I felt weighed down by toxic work relationships, and no matter what I did, nothing seemed to change.

Then one day, a friend suggested I visit a wise woman named Sharma. I sat in the quiet of her back room, sharing how I was feeling for just under an hour, before lying down for a 45-minute energy healing session. When I left, I felt like I was floating. Every light turned green on the drive home, and I walked through my front door as if levitating.

Within days, the sense of feeling stuck began to dissolve. Work problems seemed to untangle themselves, toxic partnerships ended naturally, and I felt lighter and wonderfully renewed. I kept thinking, how on earth could this be? I happened to be wearing a bio-tracker watch that records steps and heart rate. When I later checked the week's data, I was startled to see it had logged a 90-minute nap in the middle of the day. But I hadn't napped all week. Looking closer, I realised the "nap" lined up exactly with my healing session with Sharma. From the moment I entered her home my heart rate had dropped so quickly, that the device mistook it for sleep. Something profound had happened – she had induced an altered state of consciousness, and the data confirmed it.

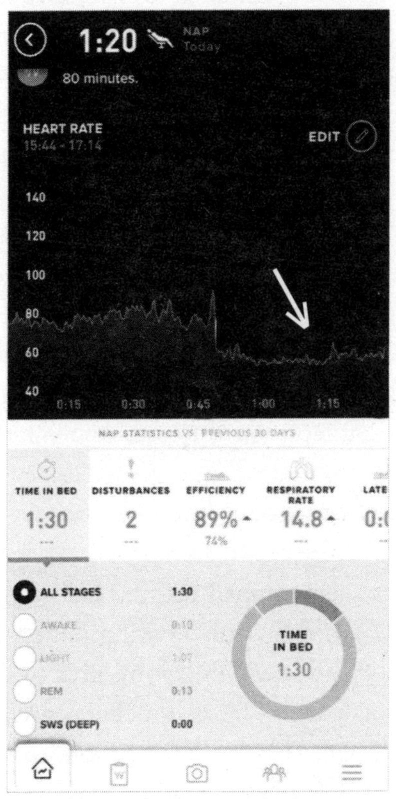

I called Sharma to find out how she had catalysed so many changes in my life. She replied, "We have four bodies: the physical, mental, emotional and spiritual. Any problems showing up in one body exists in all four bodies, and so when it comes to healing, we need to take a four-body approach. When you heal one of the bodies, changes occur in the other three."

Sharma shared a personal example of this. "Over a decade ago, I discovered a tumour growing in my neck. Of course, this wasn't just a tumour. The tumour likely began in my mind at a young age, because of the disharmony in my child-hood home from the trauma of a physically abusive father, and the constant fear that came with living in this survival mode." She explained that she had suppressed this emotional distress for decades, causing energetic stagnation that later manifested physically. Sharma continued, "The law of attraction states that we consciously or unconsciously attract more of the same, so the stress I had come to expect as a child kept coming to me in different shapes and forms in my adult life. If I hadn't changed my emotional, spiritual and mental body, my physical body would have remained attracting the same sickness."

Setting trapped emotions free

"How do you release trapped trauma before physical symptoms appear?" I asked Sharma. She explained, "My spiritual teacher, Eddie, taught me this: if you ever find yourself in a difficult situation – it can be as horrific as sexual assault or it can be as simple as frustration with a work partner, it doesn't matter, whatever it is that's bringing angst into your body – take a pen and paper and write down your deepest feelings about it for as long as you can. For me, I first wrote about losing my mum and dad, but the emotions were complicated because I loved my dad on one hand, but also watched him beat my mum several times. I had to explore this confusion, 'How dare you put your hands on her. How dare you put your hands on me.' My younger self was angry and I needed to express that, to then let go. When you can't think of anything else to write about a situation, screw those pages up. Take them outside and burn them if you can." While burning, Sharma repeats this affirmation:

I no longer need these thoughts, feelings and vibrations. I give this back to the universe and ask that it be replaced with unconditional love and healing. Please, universe, come and replace what I have released.

"Why does this help?" I asked. She responded: "During the act of journalling, I'm pulling unwanted emotional energy from my energetic aura through my arm, through the pen, to the ink on the paper. I am moving stagnant emotional memories stored in my energetic body into something two-dimensional. When I burn that, I'm transmuting that energy again into ether and I'm working with the universal laws. Another energetic law that comes into play here is the law of the vacuum, which doesn't allow space to be empty. So if I move something energetically out of myself, something will naturally flow in to fill that space. I want to have a say in the kind of energy that's going to fill that gap. I want to replace the past with unconditional love and healing. It's like breaking bad habits, if you want to stop smoking, for example, it's much easier to replace the habit with something else rather than leaving an empty void. We must always fill the space left behind with something better. I have had people miraculously recover from various conditions and reverse illnesses they had previously thought were permanent after doing their write-ups, all because their physical symptoms were based on fears or things they were holding on to that weren't serving them. And I think that's the separation that's missing for many people. They let old emotional experiences stay with them. They remain in the drama of it. It's very difficult to forgive someone when you're a volcano. So that sticky, uncomfortable energy needs to go somewhere."

Sharma's method left a deep impression on me. Healing your life force requires deepening the relationship with yourself and sealing the holes in your energetic bucket. No human goes through life unscathed. We all carry wounds. And whether they stem from heartbreak, shame or childhood pain, they quietly drain our power. Healing them isn't a luxury; it's essential. Fortunately, there are plenty of tools to help.

Breath of repair

Without realising it, Sharma had helped me enter a state of deep relaxation where healing could unfold. For thousands of years, wisdom keepers have known how difficult it is to shift biological or emotional patterns when stuck in the *mindset* that created them.

In the 1960s, one such wisdom keeper Dr Stanislav Grof[56], a clinical psychiatrist, pioneered research into how altered states of consciousness could awaken extraordinary healing potential. He first explored this through the therapeutic use of psychedelics alongside talk therapy, such as LSD, documenting how these experiences allowed patients to process what had been locked in their bodies for years and emerge with a sense of peace and wholeness. When psychedelics were banned in the late 1960s, Grof looked for alternative ways to access those deeper healing states for transformation and found it in breathwork.

Together with his wife, Christina, he developed Holotropic Breathwork, discovering that deep rhythmic breathing, evocative music and a safe environment could produce similar results. Over the course of more than 25,000 sessions, they witnessed people release deeply buried emotions, resolve long-held trauma, and access insights that talking alone could never reach. Because of the changes in oxygen and carbon dioxide levels in the blood, a gentle shift in brain activity occurs, loosening the usual boundaries of perception. The rational mind quietens, and a more intuitive intelligence takes over.

Grof believed that trauma is stored in the body as undischarged energy. When pain or fear is too overwhelming to process in the moment, its energy becomes "frozen" in the nervous system and cellular memory. The breath acts as a catalyst, reopening energetic circuits that have been historically shut down. Breath moves energy and what was frozen starts to thaw. Through this process, the body and mind have the chance to let go.

Energy release can be experienced in many ways from trembling, tears, laughter, visions, or even spontaneous movement. Grof saw this as evidence of the psyche reorganising itself. He compared it to animals in the wild that "shake off" the residue of fear after escaping a threat, nature's built-in way of returning to balance.

This type of breathwork is often described as "40 years of therapy in 40 minutes", and that's no exaggeration. I've experienced this many times myself. As the breath deepens, energy stirs, tension builds, release happens and then it all melts away. My hands often stiffen at first, as if gripping something that's finally ready to be released. The breathwork purifies your own life force.

I was so moved by the power of this technique that I encouraged my father to try it. During his session, he experienced a vision of himself as a small child being held by his mother as she shared her love for him. It was profoundly healing, offering a moment that softened a lifetime of tension.

Breathwork reveals how quickly old wounds can mend. When the body, mind and spirit move in harmony, transformation can unfold in seconds. Grof noted that these emotional releases can be so profound they must always be guided by trained practitioners.[57]

Meet me on the dance floor

Movement is one of our oldest and most effective tools for healing. Babies dance before they can speak. Rhythm is medicine; our bodies knew this before our minds could name it.

The British Medical Journal found that dancing outperformed antidepressants in treating depression[58]. While tai chi, yoga and walking helped, dance was the most transformative. I've come to understand this firsthand, as dancing has done more for my emotional healing than anything else.

Dancing doesn't just lift mood. It activates the same neural pathways used in trauma therapies like EMDR (Eye Movement Desensitisation and Reprocessing), which helps process emotions and reduce anxiety through rhythmic, bilateral movement. That's why healers and witches have danced in ritual for centuries, because rhythm releases the wounds you store and raises your frequency. Despite this clear evidence that dancing enhances personal power, less than eight per cent of adults in England move regularly.[59]

After the loss of my pregnancies, dancing was the only thing that helped me feel alive again. My body led where my words couldn't go, and slowly my energy began to return.

Group movement has even more benefits. Whether it's in a festival crowd at Glastonbury, the New Orleans Jazz Music Festival, a ritual circle, or a local club, dancing together creates energetic coherence. Boundaries dissolve, and we remember we're not alone. If communal dance is not available, you really can't go wrong with the "home nightclub trick" – lights off, music loud and "wave your hands in the air, like you just don't care". Within minutes, you'll feel a shift. Emotion starts to move and the brain begins to change.

If dancing isn't your thing, the simple act of walking forward has proven uniquely helpful for solving problems faster, generating creative ideas and recalling positive memories. How can something so simple be so powerful? It's because the brain didn't evolve to think in isolation, it evolved to think while moving – since the beginning of humanity, our minds have been shaped through physical experience. Forward motion signals progress, both literally and metaphorically, and helps the brain to focus on the future rather than the past. Just as frowning can make you feel sadder through biofeedback, walking forward can help you feel like you're moving ahead.

Sitting is truly the new smoking. Sedentary lives are harming our energetic, physical and mental health. If you are committed to healing, consciously invite movement back into your life as an internal power charger.

Top tip: Try speaking through your problems (with a friend or therapist) while walking; this can help you process emotions and events faster and with greater ease.

Stories that steal or restore your energy

Just as a sound bath can recalibrate the nervous system, the stories we tell ourselves each day resonate in ways that either drain or restore our life force.

We often think of healing as something that happens in isolated moments – a retreat, a ceremony – or a yoga class. But magic asks for something deeper, a way of living that's aware of energy at all times.

So on a daily basis, ask yourself:

- What energy am I giving away unnecessarily?
- What emotional states am I keeping myself stuck in, through the stories I keep repeating?

The words we whisper – about our worth, our past, our future, or even how we describe our days – either strengthen our energy field or weaken it.

Perhaps it's my British conditioning, but I find myself quicker to share my failures than my wins. And this isn't energetically healthy because revisiting past mistakes over and over again only depletes our energetic reservoir. There are always many ways to tell your story. I could say I was bullied by a boss who held back my career. Or I could say I found a way forward with strength and resilience, thanks to a challenging environment that taught me invaluable lessons. One version drains me. The other restores me. How can you re-tell a story that drains you?

Choosing how we tell our stories doesn't mean denying the harder chapters of our lives. Philip Carr-Gomm, a Druid teacher and psychologist, has spent much of his work exploring the relationship between story, identity and spiritual growth. He reminds us that true integration requires honesty as well as intention: "We need to 'own' as many aspects of our story as we can and not be in denial of the dark and challenging experiences we have been through. Even if we recount the story of our lives in the most positive way, it doesn't mean we are unaware of the other perspectives we could take."[60]

This kind of relationship with our past takes practice. Carr-Gomm also writes that alongside remembering ourselves, we must learn a subtler art – forgetting. "As well as owning our stories and remembering ourselves, we also need to forget parts of ourselves. In doing so, we gain clarity, become less self-preoccupied, and become of greater value and interest to others and the world."[61] In other words, energy is shaped not only by what we hold on to, but by what we choose, consciously, to lay down.

"Dance is the hidden
language of the soul."

– Martha Graham

Science yet again supports this more flexible, nuanced approach. Our memories aren't fixed records, they're reconstructions. We're biologically unable to remember a story accurately. We instead remember the gist and fill in the blanks with emotion. The Innocence Project found that in 75 per cent of wrongful conviction cases, eyewitnesses misremembered.[62] If memory is likely to be unreliable, then the past isn't a reliable source of data to draw from.

Retelling your narrative in a way that empowers you isn't denial. It's energetic hygiene. It's how we stop reactivating old pain and begin mending unnecessary leaks. You will soon start to notice how potent your magic becomes when the stories you tell recharge you.

Energy audit of stories: reclaiming your Life Force

Every story we tell carries a vibration. Some strengthen our field; others quietly siphon it. When we repeat a draining story, we keep our energy bound to the past. The practice overleaf helps you locate where your power is leaking and call it back.

Why it works: Each time you retell a story, you change how your body remembers it. Every rewritten line softens the tension the old narrative held. New stories don't just shift your perspective; they shift your physiology. They promote vitality instead of pain, transforming memory into medicine and restoring the natural flow of your life force.

Practice

Draw three columns and label them:

Story	Emotional frequency	Energy level (1–10)

1. In the first column, write the stories you often tell yourself or others about your life, especially the ones that feel heavy or defining.

   a)   *"I was in a toxic relationship for six years."*

   b)   *"I always seem to fail right before things get good."*

   c)   *"People never stay."*

2. In the second column, note the emotion that arises when you speak it aloud i.e. anger, shame, grief, exhaustion.

3. In the third, rate the energy that the story holds in your body from 1–10 (where 1 is a story that fully drains life-force energy and 10 powers it) and note where in the body you feel it most. Anything below 5 shows where your life force is caught.

4. For each low-energy story, take a deep breath and write its alchemy – a version that restores power and wisdom.

   Example: *"That relationship showed me what I don't want and how important it is for me to have a clear purpose, other-wise I can forget my own desires. My dreams are now sacred, and I will protect all the things that make me feel fulfilled."*

Protect the power within

Your energy is your magic wand. If quantum physics shows us that everything is energy – Einstein's famous $E=mc^2$ – then our moods are not just private feelings; they are energetic states, a symphony of brainwaves, hormones and heart rhythms, each with ripple effects. A bad mood alters our internal chemistry and the field we broadcast, sometimes powerfully enough to change physical reality.

To create the magic you desire, you must learn to master your moods to protect yourself from shaping a reality you don't want. This doesn't mean you can never feel tired, lost, angry or low again. It means that when you do, you actively process and alchemise the energies that weigh you down.

Charging your internal power source is not a one-time act; it's a daily devotion, a sacred relationship between you and your core. Every witch knows she needs her energy rested, nourished and regulated to work with magic effectively. It's time to tend to yours. Move it. Nourish it. Speak gently to it. Because once your energy is restored, you're no longer stuck chasing life, you're ready to draw what you want in.

And that's where we go next.

The Empress sits in her garden with a river flowing through, symbolising vibrant life-force energy, creativity and powerful manifesting skills. She embodies the divine feminine – nurturing, sensual and fertile with ideas. Associated with the planet Venus and the Earth element, the Empress signifies the power to create, to flourish and to attract wealth.

Magical seduction –
the art of magnetism

"You are a living magnet. What you attract into your life is in harmony with your dominant thoughts."

– Brian Tracy

When your energy flows freely, you move from effort to alignment, from pushing to being pulled.

Now we turn to the art of that pull: magical seduction. The words alone bubble with excitement, power and mystique. For many of us, the first things that spring to mind are romance and manipulation – but this is something completely different. Magical seduction is the practice of becoming so true to yourself that life starts to respond differently. The change doesn't happen through persuasion or trying to control a situation, but because your energy no longer clashes with what you desire.

When inner conflict dissolves, the nervous system settles, and a subtle biochemical magnetism is released. The world of vibration doesn't respond to what you wish for; it responds to who you are. "I want" doesn't get – "I am" is the key.

Acting in accord

Who is the most magnetic person you know? More often than not, we're drawn to people who are authentically themselves – those who are happily eccentric and wouldn't swap their qualities for anyone else's. This level of self-appreciation creates a radiance that is reflected back. Just as the law of cause-and-effect states: be the cause of the effect you want to experience.

Many of us, myself included, have made the painful mistake of believing that trying harder is the path to success. But, like unrequited love, the more we force it, the further it slips away. Magical seduction, however, creates the conditions for your dreams to find *you*.[63] Imagine walking into a new neighbourhood in search of food. One restaurant is buzzing with life, the other sits empty. Naturally, you are drawn to the one that feels alive. Its energy is enticing. Busy places attract more people, just as abundance within a person attracts more abundance around them. This is the mechanics of seduction. Energy is contagious and resonance is real. One yawn triggers another. One flame lights another. One vibrating tuning fork sets another humming. The signal we emit invites the same back – and the feeling we want is the one we gravitate towards.

Magical seduction, then, is not just a mindset shift but a behavioural one. The practice begins with seducing yourself – proactively fulfilling your own deepest desires and living as if they have already been met. Sounds fluffy? It's neuroscience. Action precedes emotion – in other words, it's nearly impossible to think your way into a new state of being, the brain requires actionable evidence.

This is illustrated clearly in the Benjamin Franklin effect. When Benjamin Franklin needed to win over a political opponent, he did not rely on force, argument or persuasion. He magically seduced, by asking to borrow a rare and precious book. To the opponent, the request was strange and confusing. Enemies do not ask favours of one another, and they certainly do not lend valued possessions. This is something only a "friend" would do. Lending the book required a quiet act of trust, a willingness to see Franklin as someone worthy of it. The opponent wrestled with the decision before finally agreeing. But once he did, his mind was faced with an uncomfortable contradiction. Why would he do something kind for someone he disliked and competed with? This internal tension, what psychologists call cognitive dissonance, needed resolving. And so the very act of lending shifted his emotions. "Perhaps Franklin isn't so awful after all," he thought. "Perhaps he is, in fact, a decent man." The relationship soon softened and they became friends, not because anything external changed, but because a shift in behaviour rewrote beliefs and altered dynamics.

There are countless everyday examples of this. Simply moving your body in a certain way can change how others respond to you. Smiling stimulates the brain's joy pathways and makes people perceive you as more trustworthy, agreeable and attractive.[64] Power posing, even for two minutes, can increase testosterone, giving you more confidence and perceived authority, which inspires respect. Acts of generosity light up the brain's reward circuits, releasing dopamine and oxytocin, fostering warmth and cooperation.

Magical seduction is inner power. You can't control whether someone will care for you in the future, but you can care for yourself now. You can't dictate when a promotion arrives, but you can become so excellent, they can't function without you. You can't control how attractive someone finds you, but you can nourish your body like you're a divine goddess or god, until your radiance speaks for itself. You can't demand love, but you can be lovable.

When you treat yourself as something you long for, the world naturally responds. You become tantalising. People want you. Jobs open up for you. Fun experiences seek you out. Start by curating a life that feels desirable in the *smallest* ways: take longer baths, go for slow walks, throw away socks with holes, invest in better bed sheets or spend time making food that nourishes you. And life, always listening, will answer accordingly. The moment you stop waiting for circumstances beyond your control to change, and seduce yourself instead; you become a magnet to the things you really want.

Witches have long said that if we cannot find what we seek within, we will never find it without. And in the Bible, Mark teaches that prayer works not through pleading, but through embodiment, acting as if the answer has already arrived: "Whatever you ask for in prayer, believe that you have received it, and it will be yours." (Mark 11:24)

Becoming you

The biggest barrier to magical seduction is not a lack of magic; it's a lack of self-knowledge. Traditional seduction relies on performance to secure an outcome. While this kind of manipulation may deliver short-term results, it ultimately creates long-term disconnection and dissatisfaction. Psychological research consistently shows that authenticity is a stronger predictor of wellbeing than income, education or intelligence – the very markers we are often taught to prioritise instead.[65]

Authenticity has a gravitational pull; it bends energy. Data shows us that people respond differently to truth. One study found that authentic laughter is rated as far more likeable than forced laughter.[66] Magical seduction activates when *who you are* and *how you live* are in alignment. Magic, after all, is about moving in harmony with natural forces.

I am sure everyone believes they have a "big authentic desire" to receive a lot of wealth – but if this were true, why wouldn't the universe be rearranging things accordingly? Dr Vivianne Crowley, psychologist and High Priestess of modern witchcraft, puts it perfectly when she writes, "There are too many competing psyches trying to win the lottery."[67] Her point is important: if a desire isn't truly yours, you won't have the psychic strength to sustain it. You might force something for a time, even convince yourself it's yours, but if your inner world isn't aligned enough for it to stay, life won't change. This brings me to a critical point, the reason nearly 92 per cent of people don't achieve their "goals".[68] Is the thing you want really the thing you want?

Magical seduction often gets confused with conventional manifestation. Both are concerned with creating the life you desire, but the approach is very different. Modern manifestation techniques encourage long lists of 'I wants', unconsciously shaped by external pressure, ego, or inherited ideas of success. While lists can offer clarity, they can also narrow perception, locking you into rigid outlooks and blinding you to alternative, better paths.

When identity hardens around a fixed idea of who you think you should be, over who you actually are, you become stuck chasing illusions. This is when frustration or self-blame can arise. I want reinforces lack. The more you focus on wanting something, the more your nervous system and brain register its absence. Wanting love can reinforce the absence of love, leaving you feeling empty. Wanting more money can highlight the lack of funds, making you feel poorer – a speedy ticket to extinguishing life force.

I've lost count of the times I've written ego-filled manifesting lists, trying to force desires that weren't right for me, ignoring every red flag only to eventually realise I was running after something misaligned. When you are doing everything you can to pursue something but life still isn't budging, don't deflate and assume you've failed. Instead, magical seduction invites you to reconsider who you are at your core. It swaps "why isn't this happening for me?" to "is this desire really my calling and unique gift in this lifetime?" When things don't go your way, take this as a sign to re-examine what you're striving for.

Magical seduction moves you away from craving to embodying, away from the focus on outcome to input. To master the art of the magnetic pull, you must peel away the masks you've built (we all have them), to reconnect with your sacred self. This is the purest part of you, free from other people's opinions and expectations. It is instinctual, eccentric and rooted in truth. Only when you are anchored in this level of honesty do you stop reaching for borrowed dreams. You then notice, and choose, what genuinely lights you up – and a person lit up is a person who radiates irresistible energy. I came across a line that stayed with me: "The smart ones are the people with no firm formula of who they are and instead are wildly curious about all the versions they might become."[69] It captures something essential – an openness to becoming, and this is a delicious energy to radiate.

To know yourself is the oldest wisdom and the hardest work. As Carl Jung famously shared, "The privilege of a lifetime is to become who you truly are." Our sense of self has never been under so much threat. Technology has monetised attention, using every tactic to keep us hooked on screens and media. We've never had so much choice, from what we watch to what we eat. However, all this choice leaves us more confused. Our culture pushes us towards a destructive sameness, making it harder to distinguish our own desires from those of the collective. It's alarmingly easy to fall for the illusions other people sell. Before we know it, we're chasing a version of reality that doesn't even exist. Seventy-two per cent of facial plastic surgeons report that patients now request procedures to resemble filtered versions of themselves.[70] In our search for acceptance, we follow others, believing they know the way. Yet more often than not, they're lost too. No wonder dreams struggle to unfold. It's never the magic that's absent, but the inner harmony required to wield it.

In the 1950s, psychologist Leon Festinger discovered that humans instinctively compare themselves to others to understand their own identity. In tribal settings this helped us find our role and contribution. But social media has hijacked this instinct. One scroll delivers a highlight reel of filtered perfection, stripped of context and truth. No longer can we feel special as the best baker in the tribe when there are 1.7 million "better" bakers online. The specialness we once felt in smaller communities has been taken from us, and it's highly psychologically problematic. When our sense of identity and belonging is weakened, we drift into the wrong jobs, the wrong relationships, the wrong homes. Anxiety, depression, restless thoughts and even illness eventually rise to signal that something must change. The point is: we aren't supposed to be the same. Otherness is our strength because it is our soul calling to reveal different things from one another.

The American mythologist Joseph Campbell devoted his life to studying myths and stories from cultures worldwide. He noticed a recurring pattern. Although the backdrops were

"The universe responds to who
we are, not what we say we
want. The energy you emit is
the prayer you live."

– *Marianne Williamson*

different, the same pattern emerged, and he called this *"the hero's journey"*. This narrative arc, echoed in everything from ancient epics to modern stories like *Harry Potter, Lord of the Rings* and *Legally Blonde*, charts a journey of human transformation: leaving behind the familiar, facing trials that demand growth, but ultimately returning home with deeper wisdom to share.

At some point, we all encounter this path, the moment of struggle that pushes us to rediscover who we were always meant to be. From the corporate man who eventually accepts his creative urges to be a writer, to the son or daughter tied to a family business who bravely follows their own interests, or the person who courageously embraces their real sexuality. Struggle is often the catalyst that forces you to uncover truth. That truth is the real treasure, the philosopher's stone we're all searching for.

As children, we are innately connected to our most honest selves. We act on instinct, free from self-consciousness. We sing, dance and laugh easily, embracing the world with wonder. Yet as we grow, develop a social identity and crave belonging, we are pulled away from this authenticity. Becoming yourself again is really about the *unbecoming of everything you are not*, a remembering rather than a reinvention. "The most terrifying thing is to accept oneself completely," wrote Jung[71], because doing so often means stepping apart from the crowd.

Actress Viola Davis reflected on this journey during an acceptance speech: "How silly of me not to know that I am the love of my life. I think it's because we are thrust into a world that we don't fit into. The journey is full of someone trying to sell you a bill of goods along the way. If you get some awards, you mean something; or if you go to a certain school then you've got 'it'; or if you're cute, got classical beauty, got the right man, woman, the right postcode, then you'll be worthy. You swim through all that filthy swell. Until you come to the really stark conclusion that, actually, none of it matters. You want to leave this Earth becoming who you know deep within you're supposed to be. And that transcends status. Because at the end of the day, we are here to love. The love and connection starts with self, and then you're able to share it."[72]

Her words resonate. In a world of people trying to be something else, those who want to be themselves have a quiet but mighty inner power. That is how you know someone is a witch: they dare to be fully themselves, even if it means standing alone. A witch doesn't crave acceptance. She accepts herself.

Astrology: a mystical tool for self-discovery

Magical seduction depends on authenticity and alignment, and this requires self-awareness. If you don't know who you are, you can't attract what's really yours. That is why mystics have always used tools, not to predict the future, but to remember the self. Astrology is one of the oldest mirrors we have: a map of your patterns, your gifts, and the places you leak energy trying to be someone else.

My own journey towards self-discovery began in earnest when I was 19 and met a life-changing witch (by my definition, but more accurately described as a spiritual teacher and Kabbalistic astrologer) called Ruth Nahmias. At the time, I was lost. For the previous eight years, I had been wrapped up in exactly what Viola Davis speaks of: the feeling of deep unworthiness, desperately trying – and failing – to reach the milestones I believed would bring me happiness. I was never the best at anything, nor did I have anything externally special to lean on, and this left me painfully insecure. These wounds fuelled a relentless determination to be accepted, but no matter how hard I tried, nothing quite worked out as I hoped. I needed a sign. I needed guidance. Some people turn to therapists when they feel lost, but I found myself drawn to psychics and astrologers.

Nearly 15 years later, Ruth is still one of my first calls when I feel confused. Psychoanalysis and reflection on childhood influences are undeniably valuable in helping us understand ourselves and our behaviours. But what we truly need is not to linger there for too long, but to be reminded of our capacity to transcend circumstance and history. Ruth didn't see me as I was, an insecure 19-year-old who had lost her way. She saw my soul's potential. When she read my birth chart for the first time, it was as though she held a manual to my inner workings. She described me more accurately than even my best friend could, and in ways better than I could myself. Within seconds, she could see my greatest fears, the subconscious blocks holding me back, and the areas where I needed to focus my energy for transformation.

The stars: a brief history

Astrology often invites eye rolls, yet it is older than any formal science and has served as a tool for self-exploration for millennia. While the mere mention of the topic can split a room, its enduring presence throughout history reveals just how deeply it resonates with people.

The roots of astrology stretch back to ancient Mesopotamia (modern-day Iraq) around 1800BCE, where priest-astronomers meticulously linked the patterns of heaven with the affairs of Earth. They believed celestial events reflected the will of the gods and used these signs to guide decisions in agriculture, politics and war.

In ancient Egypt, sky-watching evolved into a sacred science. Priests tracked the rising of Sirius (the "Dog Star", and brightest star of the Canis Major), whose appearance signalled the annual flooding of the Nile, and mapped 36 star groups known as decans, which later influenced the 12-sign zodiac. The heavens were alive with divine presence: Ra as the Sun, Thoth as the Moon, Isis and Osiris embodying cosmic balance.

Meanwhile, with no direct communication between cultures, a parallel system emerged in India: Jyotish, or "the science of light", rooted in the *Vedas*. Still widely practised today, the system uses the stars not only to interpret collective events, but to offer insight into an individual's karma and sacred life path. Over time, Greek and Egyptian ideas came together in Egypt's Alexandria (a meeting place of cultures) and this blend became what we now call Western astrology. Greco-Egyptian scholar Ptolemy laid the foundation for the modern birth chart, transforming astrology into a personal tool: a map of the heavens at the moment of birth that helps reveal someone's truest essence and greatest potential.

During the Middle Ages and the Renaissance, astrology was not separate from science; it *was* science. Physicians used birth charts to diagnose illness, and kings consulted astrologers before battle. The stars weren't seen as superstition but as strategy. Records show that England's King Henry VII hired Dr William Parron, an Italian astrologer, to predict political outcomes and time important events for the crown. Perhaps the most famous example of a monarch consulting the heavens is Queen Elizabeth I and her brilliant advisor John Dee (1527–1608). Dee's preserved diaries and letters reveal detailed astrological charts prepared for key royal decisions.

A mathematician, astrologer and mystic, he selected the precise date of Elizabeth's coronation according to celestial alignments, and later advised her on navigation, foreign policy and even the foundations of the British Empire.

As the Catholic Church asserted its dominance, astrology was both preserved and persecuted. Monks often studied it in secret, valuing its predictive power, while church authorities simultaneously condemned it. But, despite centuries of suppression, astrology never disappeared; a testament to its power and usefulness.

Even today, astrology invites both criticism and reverence, challenging the space between science and mysticism. This tension was brought to life in 1915, when astrologer Evangeline Adams was taken to court in New York, accused of fortune-telling, which was outlawed at the time. She was a renowned reader of the stars and famously taught the financier JP Morgan, who reportedly said, "Millionaires don't use astrology, billionaires do." The former president of the New York Stock Exchange also wrote to her in 1908 with the following:

> Dear Miss Adams, You will oblige me by seeing what the stars have for me during the consecutive months of 1908. Your forecasts for the present months were singularly correct.
> Yours truly, Jacob Stout
> Formerly President of the New York Stock Exchange

At one point, Adams was forced to defend astrology in court as a philosophical and scientific pursuit rather than mere guesswork. The case took an unexpected turn when Evangeline offered to demonstrate her abilities by casting the horoscope of someone known to the judge. With the judge's permission – and much to his surprise – she described aspects of his chosen person's personality with such accuracy that he declared astrology to be no longer punishable as superstition and instead categorised it as a branch of science.

A map back to yourself

An astrological birth chart reading is more than the general astro-babble you might find in a magazine. It maps out every planet's position at the moment of your birth, offering a far more complex and nuanced reflection of your personality, strengths, challenges, energies and archetypes. Your rising sign, like a mask you present to the world, shapes the initial impression you make on people and how others perceive you. But it also hints at the person you are becoming and the potential you're striving to unlock. Your Moon sign, residing in the realm of emotions, governs your inner world, revealing your deepest needs and how you seek comfort. Mars, the planet of action and desire, dictates how you assert yourself, pursue goals, and express your passions. Venus, the planet of love and beauty, influences your romantic style, your aesthetic preferences, and how you experience pleasure and connection.

Nothing in life is random, and most certainly, the moment your soul chose to take its first breath is not. We are intrinsically connected to the planets. After all, as we have seen, each one of us is made of stardust. Over millennia, as stars erupted into supernovae, their elements scattered across space. Those materials became new stars, planets and, eventually, people. Every atom of oxygen in our lungs, of carbon in our muscles, of calcium in our bones, of iron in our blood, shares the same cosmic ancestry as the stars before our time.

Astrology and AI

Astrology has become a tool I return to for clarity, perspective, and guidance. Since my first reading in 2010, I've made it a tradition to review my chart annually; a kind of spiritual tune-up that helps me remember who I am in a world that tries to make me forget.

The right astrologer makes all the difference. Choose wisdom over hype. A good one won't just list traits but will offer nuanced insights. I suggest finding someone with at least ten to 20 years of experience. If you prefer a self-guided approach, apps like The Pattern offer fantastically accurate interpretations.

In recent years, AI tools like ChatGPT have also become useful for exploring your chart, especially if you're just starting out. While nothing replaces a personalised session, these tools can offer surprisingly thoughtful prompts. Just be sure to double-check that your birth data and signs are correct, AI tools aren't always right.

To get started, all you need is your date, time and place of birth. From there, your chart becomes a mirror, reflecting your essence and guiding you back to your sacred self. If you can't find your exact time of birth, don't worry too much, but keep in mind that your rising sign (Ascendant) is likely to be inaccurate, as it changes roughly every two hours. The Moon can also shift signs within a day, so if you were born during a cusp period, your Moon sign may be uncertain too.

Here are five powerful prompts to explore, whether through journalling, AI or a trusted astrologer.

Who am I becoming?
Your rising sign reveals the energy you're growing in to and how others see you. Ask: *What does my rising sign say about my evolving identity?*

What do I need to feel safe and connected?
Your moon sign speaks to your emotional needs and inner world. Ask: *How does my moon sign guide my emotional well-being?*

What is my love language?
Venus and Mars shape your desires and how you love. Ask: *How do my Venus and Mars signs influence my relationships and creativity?*

What is my sacred purpose?
Your Midheaven and North Node reveal your career and soul direction. Ask: *What do my Midheaven and North Node placements say about my true calling in career and life?*

What am I here to evolve through?
Your full chart reveals karmic patterns and growth themes. Ask: *What life lessons am I here to explore and transform?*

Astrology, when approached with curiosity rather than certainty, becomes a very revealing mode of self-inquiry. And AI, when used intentionally and double-checked, can help you start that conversation. You don't have to believe everything it tells you. What matters is what it awakens. Used this way, these tools become mirrors rather than authorities, starting points that help you remember what your soul already knows.

Meet your superconscious: the home of your hopes and dreams

It's far easier for the brain to remember the past than to imagine the future. Traditional psychology often reinforces this, tracing every thought and feeling back to childhood wounds and historical events. But that story is too limiting and a threat to magnetism. We must not get stuck re-playing what has been, defining ourselves by it.

When I completed my postgraduate studies in psychosynthesis, the psychology of the soul, it challenged this psychological trap. Psychosynthesis takes the past into account, but with equal importance highlights future possibility. This was when I discovered the mind's superconscious, a lesser-known realm of the psyche where vision, hope and dreams reside.

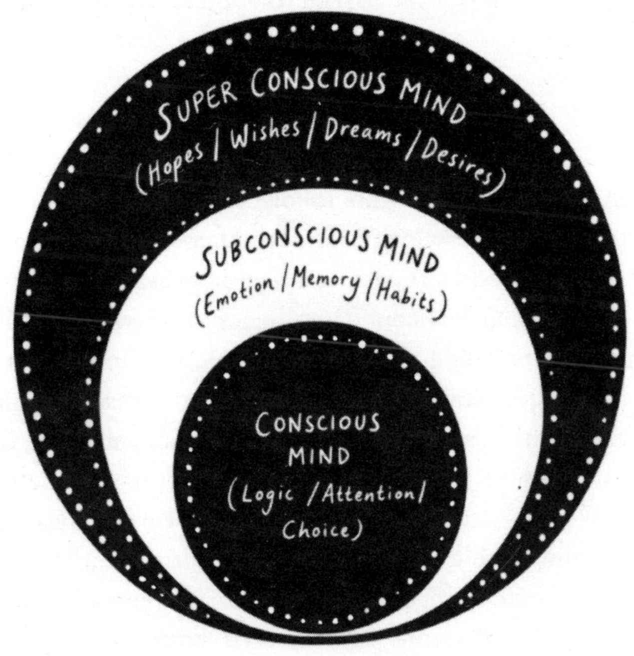

It is within the superconscious that you find your inspiration and desires, offering a sacred map to the person you want to become. When you live looking backwards, consciously or unconsciously consumed by the past, you lose connection to these divine directions. Magic doesn't flourish in the rear-view mirror; it lives in possibility and what's about to emerge.

Neuroscience affirms what mystics know: dwell in pain and your mind is wired to find more of it. Dwell in vision and your world rearranges to meet it. Your filter system (the RAS) will always rearrange to spot evidence that supports the dominant focus.

Look at Oprah Winfrey, Steve Jobs or Nelson Mandela – lives born from hardship yet redirected into brilliance. If our past truly defined us, none of their transformations would have been possible. They strengthened their superconscious, the home of future vision. We all have the same magical choice: which part of the psyche will you let lead you?

Three steps to strengthen your superconscious

Fortune favours those who follow their authentic desires. When the superconscious is strong, life's setbacks and fears don't strike as deeply. A clear connection to who you want to become at a soul level builds resilience. Real optimism isn't formed in pretending everything will succeed and giving up when it doesn't. Real optimism is finding a sacred calling and knowing that, despite what happens, this is the song your soul came here to sing.

1. Get comfortable with desire
Desire has been shamed for too long. Across centuries, we've been told it's dangerous, selfish, even sinful. But it wasn't

always this way. In ancient wisdom traditions, desire was revered as holy, like a divine compass. It was seen as the flame of life itself, the spark that awakens *heka* – creation and your calling. When desire is suppressed, the consequences are far-reaching. It doesn't just dim life's magic; it severs you from your truth. To exile desire is to exile your own inner guidance.

Desires are mystical because we don't choose them; they spontaneously arrive often without a logical reason. Some people desire to travel the world, others to build a home. Some feel called to invent a water system; others to sing on stage. Desire is deeply personal, inexplicable, often illogical and very magical. Understanding your desires is essential to finding fortune. Contrary to popular conditioning, fortune isn't about amassing power through things you don't even want. It's about locating a deep inner power – one that brings a rich, sustaining joy, capable of carrying you through real suffering. This is why someone who loves plants may feel infinitely more fortunate as a gardener than they ever would chasing a corporate title, even if the paycheck is smaller.

"Be who God meant you to be, and you will set the world on fire," wrote the Italian mystic St Catherine of Siena in the 13th century.[73] She expresses a universal spiritual truth: that when we each *fully inhabit our soul's purpose*, we naturally illuminate and transform the world around us. The joy we radiate reverberates outwards and returns to us amplified. At its heart, this is seduction – to tend your own light so brightly that it calls the world to meet it.

At first, it might seem selfish to follow desire, but really, it's an act of sharing. When you do, your energy field becomes deliciously electric, and that energy is contagious. Humanity is at risk of falling deaf to its own calling and desperately needs the voices within it, to wake it up. Be someone who reminds others how joyful life can be when it's lived authentically.

Eccentric people are magical – they ooze a self-acceptance and life-force energy that makes you fall back in love with being alive.

Explore your desires

Desire cannot be controlled or summoned on command. It isn't productive, and it doesn't respond well to pressure, deadlines or obsessive control. Desire is a cosmic force that requires patience and time to dream.

We each carry a soul code, a calling that's ours alone, and it's our responsibility to uncover it. It doesn't have to be grand or world-changing; even revealing one true thing about yourself can open the door to an entirely new experience of life.

- Which desire feels most alive in you right now – even if it doesn't make logical sense? *(Let your soul answer, not your to-do list.)*
- How might honouring this desire uplift not just you, but those around you? *(Explore the ripple effect of your aliveness.)*
- If you trusted that this desire was divinely placed within you, what would your next step be?
- What came effortlessly to you as a child? What did your soul love to do before you knew the word "should"? What did you do with ease and wonder?

2. Create a magical vision and find your expanders

One of the most effective ways to explore deeper desires and strengthen this part of your psyche is by creating a magical vision – a future mental picture that excites and expands what's possible. This isn't about writing a shopping list or setting rigid goals. It's about getting comfortable with a future life that feels authentically aligned and has the power to keep you going.

One way to expand your sense of possibility is to notice living examples around you. Mystical teacher Lacy Phillips calls them "expanders", people who embody the dreams you hold. An expander might be a friend whose relationship radiates the love you long for, a colleague who brings freedom and creativity into their work, or someone who walks with the grounded confidence you admire. When self-doubt whispers that your deepest desires are out of reach, expanders stand as living proof that they are not. And the fact that, out of billions of people, you noticed this person is not random. Their life carries a message meant for you, a reminder that yes, you can too.

Science yet again echoes this mystical technique. Psychologists describe it as "social learning theory",[74] we learn not only through our own experience but by witnessing others. Neuroscience shows this too. We learn by watching. When we see someone else grow, our brain releases chemicals linked to motivation and belief. Their expansion subtly changes our inner chemistry, helping us feel that a bigger life is possible for us too.

Who expands your perspective of what's possible?

Magical vision – guided visualisation

A magical vision is a useful exercise in helping you strengthen your superconscious. By entering deep relaxation, an altered state of consciousness emerges, allowing you to go deeper than a surface-level manifesting shopping list:

1. Close your eyes and take a deep, slow breath into your belly.
2. Breathe in through the nose for a count of five, and out through the mouth for a count of five.
3. Repeat for ten full belly breaths, letting your shoulders soften, your jaw unclench and your mind quiet with each exhale.
4. When you feel sufficiently relaxed, imagine you are walking through a beautiful wood, several years from now. The air is fresh and fragrant, sunlight dapples through the leaves, and you feel entirely at peace. In this moment, you are the happiest, most fulfilled version of yourself.
5. Notice how your future self moves. What's their posture like? The expression on their face? The light in their eyes?
6. With this image in your mind's eye, begin to connect with them more deeply by asking:
   – Where are you living?
   – What does your home feel like?
   – How do you spend your mornings?
   – What kind of work or projects fill your days?
   – Who shares your life?
   – What kinds of relationships do you nurture?

– What brings you joy and meaning?

– What are you learning or exploring right now?

– How do you care for your body and your energy?

– What values guide your choices?

– What is one piece of wisdom you want to remember today?

Pause after each question to let the answers emerge naturally – through images, sensations, words or feelings. There's no need to force anything; simply allow your future self to reveal what you most need to know.

7. When you're ready, slowly return to the present, journalling the insights, feelings and clarity you've just received.

As you move through this, remember, you're not looking for logic, you're looking for that fuzzy, truth-tingling feeling. That's your superconscious speaking. That's when you know you've tapped into a vision that's yours.

3. Find inspiration for desire in unlikely places

Despite its romantic name, magical seduction is really a technique for every area of life, because at its core, it's about embodiment and activating energy. That said, it can be exquisitely powerful when navigating love and relationships.

Most of us have been there – had a crush on someone who didn't feel the same way. It's ego-bruising to say the least. But often, what we crave or idealise in another person isn't really about *them*; it's about us and what our desires reveal about our own psyche. More specifically, it's about the parts of ourselves we've forgotten, denied or long to develop. We are all vulnerable to projecting these inner energies outwards onto romantic crushes, fantasy partners, mentors, or even people who trigger us. We fall for them, chase them or obsess over them not because they complete us, but because they mirror something we haven't yet claimed within.

In Jungian psychology, these archetypal inner energies are known as the *Anima* and *Animus*, the inner feminine and masculine aspects of the psyche. The Animus embodies qualities like clarity, logic and self-trust; the Anima expresses emotion, creativity, sensitivity and intuition. When these aspects remain unconscious or underdeveloped, we seek them outside ourselves, mistaking projection for connection.

I had to learn this the hard way.

I was desperately trying to make an unrequited crush like me. Despite my meticulous strategy, nothing worked. No matter how much I tried, nothing changed – I was left waiting for a text, an invitation; delusionally daydreaming about what our lives could be like together. I sought advice from Deike. Her answer was unexpected: "You need to internalise him – he is your *animus*, your inner man." She continued, "All rejections and romantic crushes provide valuable insight into what you *truly desire*. They can be wonderful accelerators in personal development. The qualities you admire in someone else are unrealised qualities and desires within yourself – you wouldn't be able to notice them otherwise. Maybe it's time to develop the qualities you crave in this person and strengthen the 'man of one's own.'" I knew I admired my crush's sense of confidence, his ability to make me laugh, his self-trust and security – qualities I felt I lacked. Perhaps he really was just a reflection of my *Animus*.

As I pondered this further, I realised I did desire these traits. My feelings of rejection from this crush didn't need to damage my self-esteem; instead, they could become an inspired pathway to better understand my deeper soul wants. Deike's perspective shifted me away from obsessing over acquiring things externally, such as a new perfect boyfriend, to focusing on integration and becoming the person I wanted to be. After working on embodying my inner man for a matter of months and consciously integrating these qualities, a new, fulfilling relationship found me.

Sara, a wise witch I met for coffee, shared a similar journey in developing her superconscious post-divorce. "It took me ten years to understand that a good relationship has nothing to do with anyone else," she said. "I wrote a list of everything I wanted in a partner, and then I realised that these were the qualities I needed to develop in myself." Within a few months, she unexpectedly met the love of her life at a local bar. The philosophy of magical seduction – embody, become, seduce – is the greatest secret available to all of us.

The same technique for utilising rejection for maximum seduction power applies when you're feeling jealous. Envy is a gift because it reveals what you truly desire, but might not yet recognise or feel worthy of. We all have those people in our lives who annoy us disproportionately. Instead of jumping to judgment or critique, try seeing them less as triggers and more as teachers. They're magical breadcrumbs in disguise, revealing the holes you need to fill.

Carl Jung once said, "Everything that irritates us about others can lead us to an understanding of ourselves."[75] In other words, envy isn't a problem; it's a portal.

> ## Jealousy lights the way
>
> Think about who makes you green with envy, and ask yourself:
>
> 1. What qualities can I admire about the person who triggers me the most?
> 2. Is there something within myself I'm being called to develop?

A reminder

The poet Marina Tsvetaeva once wrote, "my whole life is a romance with my own soul"[76] – this is the level of devotion to your true self you need to make life magnetic. If you chase butterflies, they will fly away. But if you build a beautiful garden, the butterflies will come to you effortlessly. And if they don't, you still have a lovely garden. That's how seduction works. When you seduce yourself first, beliefs shift, the law of resonance activates, and more of the same energy is drawn towards you. You become the cause of the effect you want to experience.

A person honouring their unique desires hums at an enchanting frequency. Over the years, I have noticed that every witch who walks that path has felt different to other people. Their energy was so authentic, eccentric and wonderfully fulfilled, that it was impossible to miss. They weren't asking for an invitation into someone else's world. They had us all wanting to be in theirs.

That is magical seduction.

"A feminist is any
woman who tells the
truth about her life."

– *Virginia Woolf*

The Tower card represents sudden upheaval. It tears down illusions, forcing us to confront truth, release attachments, and evolve. Like the diamond formed under intense pressure, the Tower's chaos isn't punishment – it's the necessary breakdown before new things can arrive. The fall is never the end, it's the beginning of transformation.

Think like a diamond

"The word 'crisis' is from the Greek, meaning 'a moment to decide'. The recurrent moments of crisis and decision, when understood, are growth junctures, points of initiation which mark a release from one state of being and a growth into the next."

– Jill Purce[77]

When life doesn't unfold the way you hope, it's easy to lose faith in magic and your own seductive power. When hardship strikes, it stirs fear, anxiety, frustration and even anger. Like clouds obscuring the sun, your inner landscape darkens, and it feels as though the universe has stopped winking at you.

But here's one certainty: chaos and disorder will happen. It's a fundamental law of nature. Physicists call it entropy, the tendency of every system to break down, so that new patterns can emerge. Change is not an interruption of life's magic, but it's very engine. We should not fear it, but embrace disorder as nature's way of progression.

So how do you stay radiant when crisis strikes? By radiating your inner diamond: forged under immense pressure,

"You will not always be loved, Alice. There will be days when others will be tired and bored with life, have their heads in the clouds, and hurt you. Because people are like that, they somehow always end up hurting each other's feelings, whether through carelessness, misunderstanding, or conflicts with themselves. If you don't love yourself, at least a little, if you don't create an armour of self-love and happiness around your heart, the feeble annoyances caused by others will become lethal and will destroy you. The first time I saw you, I made a pact with myself: 'I will avoid loving you until you learn to love yourself.'"

– Unknown

shaped by fire … only through its cuts does it learn to refract the full spectrum of light and become valuable. In the same way, your challenges can refine you.

It's time to get savvier in moments of crisis. If the universe longs for equilibrium, think two steps ahead: your actions now shape what unfolds later. This kind of tactical awareness places you back in a position of power. The key to emotional freedom is what Dion Fortune defined as magic: the art of changing consciousness at will. The ability to choose how you feel and act in any given moment, no matter what you are facing. It may not be easy, but it is the most exquisite magic you can cultivate.

The optimistic witch: the art of looking forward

Fortune favours the bold witch. When we learn to process and even welcome change, we open ourselves to infinite magic. Change, though it can feel threatening, is often the gateway to greater alignment. Just as the seasons change or the snake fearlessly sheds its skin in anticipation of renewal, we, too, can release what no longer serves us. We must lean into the natural laws of change that arrive on our doorstep, whether they're welcome or not. The tree doesn't mourn the loss of its leaves or try to stop them from dropping; it simply enters a period of stillness, knowing that, in time, it will regenerate and prepare for a new spring.

Deike lives by this magical philosophy: "You never know what's around the corner. But for me, that's always hopeful. I'm always waiting for the next good thing to come up. When something falls down, I wonder what better experience will take its place." She is a living example of a diamond mentality. She's been married three times in the course of her wonderful

80 years, and her third husband was the best, the true love of her life, a soul mate in every sense of the word. Deike's optimism is contagious. She has shown me that expecting positive outcomes in the face of uncertainty and disruption only opens the brain to more opportunities, and thus magic. She suggests using this mantra to help strengthen the shiny thinking:

> I don't know what's around the corner, but I trust it can only be good.

Studies support her optimistic view. Divorce is one of the most stressful human experiences and nearly one in three marriages end this way. But data shows that 67 per cent of divorcees remarry[78] – clear evidence that a breakdown is not the end. It's easy to get stuck mourning what you've lost, but most likely, you're on the cusp of gaining so much more. It just hasn't been revealed yet. That's why this magical mindset is essential. It reminds us that a brighter future is possible, even if we can't see it yet. Trust in the invisible is key, new possibilities can only rise from the collapse of the old.

As I write this chapter, David Bowie's song "Changes" has just started playing in the coffee shop where I'm sitting. Another perfect synchronous moment! The universe is winking at me, ushering me to heed the words I write.

Cause, effect and the magic word: pause

Pausing is one of the most important skills to master when thinking like a diamond. As a naturally impulsive person, I've found it difficult to learn, but every time I manage it, the effect is transformative. The pause is the difference between being the magician, staying in your power, or the manipulated audience, caught in subservience.

When we react blindly to triggers, as our basic biology encourages, we give up our magic wand to navigate life on our own terms. From the annoying traffic jam that spikes our stress to the "incompetent" colleague who takes over our thoughts, to frustration at politicians, or anything that makes life not go our way, we become pawns in someone else's game. But by stepping back and making space, we move from being the chess piece to the chess player. Pausing allows us to shift our energy, and our experience of reality.

After one of those weeks where everything felt like it was falling apart, a kabbalistic teacher called Yaeli asked me, "Poppy, were you the cause or the effect this week?" I didn't know what she meant until she explained: "You can only ever be the cause of a situation, or the effect – the consequence of it. Let's say your partner arrives home in a terrible mood and this annoys you. Someone else's negativity has created yours. Your partner is the cause of the energy, and you're the effect. Living as the effect is exhausting. It leaves you out of control, open to being hit by anyone else's emotional waves, and waves that have nothing to do with you."

I was stunned. I thought back to all the times I'd felt hijacked by someone else's stress. My business partner was ruining my mood. My partner's anxiety became my anxiety. I was spiralling over emails that hadn't been replied to. I was one big ball of stress – reacting to everything and everyone around me.

This is why Dione Fortune's definition of magic – "the ability to change consciousness at will"[79] – is one I return to so often. It captures the essence of true magic, which, far from being about superstition, is the skill of mastering one's inner state. Your magic is only as strong as your emotional steadiness. Emotional instability weakens your energetic focus. We must practise being the cause of how we feel, not the effect of our environment. And pausing is the gateway to this shift.

Ironically, challenges offer the perfect training ground for this. They ask you to choose: will you pause and reclaim your power, or get swept up in impulsive reactions?

Emotions are a key source of information, but they're not always intelligent. Neuroscience confirms this: when our emotional centre (the amygdala) is triggered, it takes a moment longer for the wise, rational centre of our brain (the prefrontal cortex) to come online. Pausing allows that wisdom to catch up. Emotions are loud, and intuition is quiet, so space is necessary for your soul to speak.

The next time your partner or a colleague is in a bad mood, pause. Be the cause. Don't let their energy knock you out of alignment and take your power. Choose to not react and, instead, read something beautiful. Play a song that soothes you. Protect your frequency like it's your most sacred possession – because it is.

The power to pause becomes even more valuable when life seriously alters in ways you didn't choose. Unwanted changes are often the root of the deepest emotional pain, and so we learn to fear change. But, as my mother used to say, "worrying about change is like being a bird on a branch, terrified it will snap, forgetting you have wings". The most magical people I know slow life down by using the power of pause to remember those wings. Most of us cling to the familiar – jobs, relationships, patterns – even when they hurt us. Ironically, what we call a "comfort zone", is often anything but. But when we take a beat to reconnect to wisdom, change becomes a sacred invitation.

To practise the magical pause is to practise emotional

autonomy. It's not about denying feelings; it's about holding off from responding impulsively so you can act with intention. Every challenge is an opportunity: will you stay anchored in your magic and control what happens next, or be controlled by what enters your field?

Pause is the first spell you ever need to learn.
Pause is where miracles begin.

Magical reflection: are you the cause of your life or the effect of others?

Take a moment to check in with yourself. When emotions rise or things don't go your way, ask yourself these questions, and note down:

- Am I choosing my response or reacting out of habit?
- Is this emotion mine or have I absorbed it from someone else?
- Right now, am I acting like the magician or the audience?
- What would my truest self do in this moment?
- When was the last time I let someone else's mood dictate mine?
- What might have changed if I had paused and protected my frequency instead?

The universe's unexpected gifts

The irony of disaster is that it's often the beginning of the best thing that's ever happened to you. During many of my small and big life disasters, Kabbalistic teacher Monica Berg has reminded me, "When you feel confused, lost, or uninspired, this is a sign that the next level of your life is craving to be revealed. Emotional discomfort is like soreness after a good workout – it signals growth." Think about what's happened after some of your hardest moments, what unexpected blessings came to be? For me, I usually come up with my next business idea after a period of feeling lost and exhausted. The pain and discomfort typically spark my most effective creativity.

This is one of life's great paradoxes. We panic at the thought of falling down, but the biggest miracles are usually waiting for us at the bottom. One of my oldest friends, spent over 15 years chasing his dream of becoming a singer. He was beaten down, disappointed and on the brink of giving up. His talent was undeniable; everyone saw it. So why wasn't his dream coming true? Eventually, financial stress forced him to take a break from music. He needed a way to make money, so he started gardening. Three months later, something incredible happened. Seemingly out of nowhere, a song he'd written years earlier was picked up by one of the biggest pop stars in the world. The single was an instant hit, and his bank balance skyrocketed to numbers he could never have imagined. His story is a perfect reminder that the universe often has a plan far greater than our own. Sometimes, the door we keep knocking on isn't meant to open until we take a different path, one that leads to something even better. When you embrace the idea that the greatest wonder is found after a period of darkness, challenging times feel less scary. "If you are going through hell, this is a good thing," say the Kabbalists. For these wisdom teachers, difficulty is the clearest sign that a profound gift is waiting for you. If you're experiencing emotional, physical or spiritual struggle, remember that discomfort means you're in the spiritual gym, working towards magic and miracles. No pain, no growth.

Sometimes, the greatest act of magic is in allowing things to unfold even when they arrive uninvited. This doesn't mean being passive, but rather trusting that there is a greater plan always at play. As philosopher Friedrich Nietzsche wrote in 1888:

> My formula for greatness in a human being is *amor fati*: that one wants nothing to be different, not forwards, not backwards, not in all eternity. Not merely bear what is necessary, still less conceal it […] but love it.

To love a fate we'd rather reject is a hard ask. But if we believe everything is guiding us towards something better, it becomes easier to meet what happens with radical acceptance and grace, even when it doesn't make sense in the moment.

Social media can create the illusion that everyone is constantly "doing", always in motion, always achieving, always getting what they want. But don't fall for it. Life moves in cycles. Maybe you're in a metaphorical winter, a season of rest, reflection and rebuilding. Or perhaps you're in summer, ready to play, be present and take action. Each phase has its own purpose. The interplay between waiting and acting is part of the cosmic rhythm we must all learn to navigate.

Challenges from other lifetimes

If you're feeling disheartened that life keeps going "wrong" despite how hard you try, this piece of magical insight might offer the clarity you need. Monica introduced me to the ancient Kabbalistic wisdom of *tikkun*, which teaches that each soul enters this world with a unique mission – to grow, evolve and overcome a predetermined sequence of hardships. According to this perspective, the difficulties you face aren't random, they're precisely and perfectly tailored to guide your soul's elevation in the most meaningful way for you. Nothing arrives in life by chance; the soul chooses its parents as the perfect vessels for its journey and players of its divine curriculum. Furthermore, you did not come here only to be safe or happy but to risk everything to live a life that is true to you.

Kabbalists say, "Your biggest challenge is your biggest *tikkun*." By working through it, you fulfil your soul's purpose and lift not only yourself, but the entire world. Understanding your *tikkun* is a powerful tool for revealing the deeper "why" behind life's disruptions. For example, someone deeply attached to power or wealth might find their greatest challenges arise through a loss of status, failure, or being constantly surrounded by people who appear more successful. These experiences can feel like direct threats to identity and self-worth. But they are not punishments, they're perfectly designed divine invitations for this person to loosen their grip on superficial attachments and choose authenticity. If such a person were to make different decisions based on more truthful values, they'd open an even bigger stream of blessings.

Another example: someone whose journey involves learning self-worth may repeatedly find themselves in toxic or unfulfilling relationships. On the surface it feels like life is working against them, but the deeper, divinely designed invitation is to face the fear of loneliness and cultivate inner fulfilment first. Each heartbreak becomes less a setback and more a stepping stone towards a different future.

The ancient Kabbalists believed our *tikkun* is shaped by past-life choices and unresolved patterns. So, when life doesn't unfold as planned, or manifestations don't arrive on time, don't rush to blame yourself. You might simply be working through karmic echoes of cause and effect from previous lifetimes. The key is to keep moving forward and look for the soul lesson hidden inside the chaos. The quicker you unlock the lesson, the quicker the challenge disappears.

Furthermore, if you witness someone seemingly "getting away" with unjust behaviour with no sign of *tikkun*, remember: the karmic balance sheet isn't limited to this lifetime. "We are making the conditions for our next life now, though in the present, we have to take all or part of the karma left from our last one," writes Dion Fortune.[80] Rest assured, karma always pays attention because the lore of cause and effect is forever in process. No one gets away with unjust actions.

So how do we meet these sacred challenges with grace? How do we honour our *tikkun*, alchemise karma and step into greater harmony and magic? The answer will be different for each of us. Your soul's assignment is uniquely yours, and so is the path that will set it free.[81]

How to solve tikkun *and elevate quicker*

After first learning about Tikkun, I immediately wanted to understand how to accelerate through my unique life lessons and wondered whether it was possible to avoid them altogether (I imagine you're asking the same question)! No human wants to stay in discomfort for one minute more than they must. Monica had the answer: restriction. The word restriction reminds me of the feeling that arises when you know you shouldn't have the third helping of chocolate cake, but you just really want it. Annoying! Soul restriction is slightly more nuanced, but it is a life-changing magical tool.

"*Amor Fati* is a mindset.
It's the practice of accepting
everything that happens –
good or bad – as necessary.
That it had to happen
for you to become you."

– Ryan Holiday

It is the act of going against your natural will and habits. For example, restriction for a people-pleaser would be to say no when someone asks them for something. But restriction for someone who is self-interested would be having to say yes and give generously. Restriction for a type A – a highly controlling personality who likes to bulldoze into situations – would be to slow down and ask themselves questions like: how can I approach this more gently? How can I be open to doing things differently and listening to others more? But restriction for a type-B personality – someone who procrastinates, delays action and waits for the "perfect" moment – would be to act in a more type-A way and push forward. Depending on your natural tendencies, spiritual restriction invites you to do the opposite of what comes easily, to stretch beyond habit for the sake of evolution. Someone who's money-obsessed might practise restriction through charity or acts of service. Someone deeply spiritual might find growth in focusing more on material needs. Restriction creates expansion and light. Just as striking a match needs friction, good fortune is born from moments of resistance.

Whether you're pushing forward or learning to let go, the important thing is that you're moving, evolving, and embracing change – that is our soul mission. Experiment with your restriction, pause your auto-pilot reactions and question, how could I challenge life slightly differently? (Even if a new way makes you uncomfortable.) Albert Einstein famously said, "The definition of insanity is doing the same thing, expecting a different result." Spiritual restriction helps you to avoid doing just that, creating space for something better to emerge.

Explore your karmic lessons in this lifetime

One of the best ways to gain insight into your karmic lessons in this lifetime is to explore your North and South Node placement within your astrological birth chart.

These lunar nodes are closely linked to the concept of *tikkun*, your soul's evolutionary path. Your South Node represents the qualities, talents and patterns you've already mastered – either from past lives or early life conditioning.

This is the energy you're most comfortable in but also the one that can keep you stuck if overused. The North Node, on the other hand, points to the unfamiliar but transformative path your soul is meant to walk. It often feels uncomfortable or foreign at first, yet it holds the key to growth, alignment, and soul fulfilment.

If you're curious about what this means for you and don't have access to an astrologer you trust, explore using AI. All you need is your birth date, time and location. (NB: Please double-check your birth time and location so that your planet placements are correct before you let AI interpret anything. Nodes move quite slowly, so if you don't know your birth time, it's still possible to get an accurate result.) Here's how to begin.

Prompt 1:
Either use an astrology app or ask: "Can you calculate my North and South Node placements? My birth date is [insert date], I was born at [insert time] in [insert city, country]."

Once you have your node placements, ask your AI tool to explain their meanings.

Prompt 2:

"What does it mean if my North Node is in [sign] and my South Node is in [sign]? Please explain the soul lessons and personal growth themes associated with this axis."

Prompt 3:

"What habits, skills or psychological patterns am I likely carrying from my South Node in [sign] and how might they be limiting me?"

Prompt 4:

"What are some daily practices or mindset shifts that could help me move towards the qualities of my North Node in [sign]?"

Prompt 5:

"How do my lunar nodes influence my life purpose or calling, and how can I work with this awareness to create more alignment in my relationships/career/personal development?"

These prompts offer a meaningful way to begin exploring your karmic blueprint. Of course, I still believe there's no substitute for a skilled human reader, especially one trained in karmic or evolutionary astrology. But this is an empowering and accessible second option.

Like diamonds forged through the earth's deepest pressure, our souls are sculpted through moments of intensity, heartbreak and upheaval. Magic doesn't promise a painless path – it offers a lens to see purpose in the chaos. The universe is not punishing you – it's preparing you. To think like a diamond is to remember that life's interruptions are part of a sacred alchemy: polishing us into our truest form.

Life will always bring storms, but when you choose to pause, to feel, and still to choose your own frequency, that is power. Even if you are in chaos, you can still shape the energy. That is transformation. When you choose curiosity over control, you don't just endure change, you metabolise it. This is magic.

"We win our freedom by
learning the lessons life forces on
us; and if we refuse, they become
more and more drastic."

– *Dion Fortune*

Physics tells us that energy cannot die, only transform. So is death an ending, or a doorway? The death card may look scary, but if you look closely, the Sun is about to rise. Symbolically, this card teaches us that death is a process of transformation, paving the way for the dawn to come.

Make peace with death —
the most magical transition of all

"Birth isn't a beginning and death isn't an ending. They are merely points on a continuum."

– Elisabeth Kübler-Ross[82]

Death is the greatest challenge we face, and the one we most fear. Sometimes it shows up as dread of our own mortality, or as the grief of losing someone we love. We also encounter it in smaller ways: the death of the ego through failure, embarrassment or rejection. Yet the mystics, healers and witches I've met on this journey speak of death with reverence. They see it not as an ending, but as a threshold in the ongoing process of transformation and soul evolution. As one pagan herbalist put it to me: "Just life, death, rebirth, over and over again."

Our attitudes towards death have shifted dramatically in response to changing cultural, religious and scientific perspectives. Historically, death was often seen as a passage to another realm, as evidenced by prehistoric burial sites and the elaborate tombs of ancient Egypt, where offerings were left to accompany the deceased on their journey into the afterlife. Birth and death were communal events. People were born and died surrounded by family and friends who played active roles in supporting arrivals and departures. Wise women, witches and midwives attended to both the living and the dying, offering practical assistance and comfort during these pivotal moments. Death was familiar; its sights, sounds and rituals were part of everyday life.

However, as time progressed and science began to dominate our cultural lens, the approach to death shifted. With the rise of the Enlightenment and the increased reliance on medicine and hospitals, death was moved out of the home and into institutions, where families no longer played a central role. Death became something that happened behind closed doors, its rituals hidden away. World War I intensified this suppression, with deaths occurring far from home and "Keep Calm and Carry On"-style propaganda discouraging public displays of grief. Over time, death became something fearful, distant and clinical, detached from the spiritual and transformative significance it had once held. As society has silenced death, we have also cut ourselves off from the wisdom it has to offer, the cycles of life and renewal that are central to magical living. To truly understand life, we must also understand death. Reconnecting with ancient perspectives reminds us that death is not an ending, but part of a continuum – a turning of the great wheel that carries us from one form into the next.

My own perspective on death began to change one summer afternoon. It was July 19th, 2018 – my birthday. I had booked a healing appointment as a way to find peace amidst the stress I was feeling. Living in Los Angeles, far from family and friends, I was homesick. Birthdays can be emotional at the best of times, and I spent most of the morning crying. By the time I arrived at the healer Muraid's house, I was emotionally drained.

Muraid greeted me with a warm smile, and her energy immediately soothed me. After a few gentle questions, she wrapped me in crisp white sheets for an energy healing session. I wasn't sure what to expect, but as soon as the session began, I slipped into a deep sleep. An hour passed, and I woke with no memory of what had happened. As I sat up, Muraid smiled and said, "there's an old man with us with white, slightly curly hair and a middle-aged woman with dark hair standing behind you. They're in the sea, splashing around and waving. Do you know them?" I knew exactly who they were: my grandfather Poppa and my aunt Sarah. They had passed away a few years before but there they were, happy, playing in the water. The sea had always been their favourite place. Muraid continued, "They want you to know they're happy and together. They're smiling and playing in the waves." At that moment, something shifted within me. My understanding of death began to evolve. Maybe it wasn't the end, but simply a "see you later".

After the session, I shared the news with my mother that Poppa and Sarah had visited. As tears rolled down our cheeks, we both knew this was a message, not just for me, but for her too. That moment planted the seed for my deeper exploration of death and rebirth.

In magical living, death isn't feared but respected and embraced as a doorway to transformation and an opportunity to release and evolve. As a medicine woman said to me, "Without death, life would be so boring and pointless. The best thing you can do is live fully, learn from your mistakes, and look forward to what comes next." We have a choice: to meet loss with fear and denial or to prepare for it as another step in our soul's eternal journey. Magical living chooses the latter.

Beyond the veil

Near-death experiences (NDEs) provide fascinating insights into the continuity of life after death. Beginning in 1965, Dr Raymond Moody conducted extensive interviews with over 150 individuals who had been pronounced clinically dead but returned to life.[83] He studied NDEs from people of various ages, genders, backgrounds and religious beliefs, who had all died momentarily under different circumstances, such as cardiac arrest, traumatic accidents or during surgery. Despite the variation, the accounts of what each person experienced were remarkably similar. Recurring themes included out-of-body experiences, tunnels of light, meeting past loved ones, reliving events in a panoramic fashion, feelings of calm and joy, and a reluctance to return because the experience felt so peaceful. They nearly all reported a profound change in consciousness on awakening, and that any fear of the end had vanished. Instead, they were left with a deep understanding that death was just a transition to another state of being.

I've now spoken to a few people who have experienced near-death experiences (NDEs), and their accounts consistently echo Dr Raymond Moody's observations. One of them, intuitive healer Katrina Flokis, momentarily died while giving birth. When she returned to consciousness, she discovered she had gained the ability to see people's energy fields, and, remarkably, the capacity for "future-seeing", or psychic insight.

To understand this further, I interviewed Marielle Ford Clark, a spiritual midwife who helps people approach death with greater peace. She shared her own NDE in 1992 with me: "I died on the operating table and was pronounced dead. I found myself floating out of my body and into the most magnificent, light-filled space. I had the most amazing journey into the afterlife, into somewhere that felt like heaven. It was so beautiful, so peaceful. The music I heard, the grace, the symphony of undiluted love I felt was so pure. I will never forget it. And then this hand came out through this beautiful golden light, like a stop sign. And it said, 'no, you can't cross, you can't come any further'." This moment changed everything for Marielle. Before it, she had been deeply unhappy; after it, her life took on a clear purpose: to help others learn how to die well.

One of the people Marielle began to help was her friend's daughter, Lucy, who had been diagnosed with leukaemia at nine. And although Lucy underwent a successful bone marrow transplant, she had sadly relapsed three years later. "The prognosis was grim," Marielle explained. "She was told she had only weeks to live. Lucy drifted in and out of consciousness. At one point, she suddenly woke up, tapped her mum's hand, and exclaimed, 'Mummy, I've been in the most beautiful place. I've been playing with Peter, and he told me to tell you, you are not to be sad for me. He's going to come for me soon, and he'll take care of me on the other side.' The incredible thing is that Lucy never knew she had a brother named Peter; he had died three years before she was born, and her mum had never told her. The reassurance this brought was immeasurable."

When I asked Marielle why she thought she was sent back after her NDE when others weren't, she paused and said, "Every soul chooses its timing … its reason for coming, whether it's for a season, a reason or a lifetime. It could be as short and brief as a baby in its mother's womb. I bless anybody who has had miscarriages like myself, but sometimes the soul just needed to be in the mother's womb to touch the Earth plane to complete a sacred contract they had." In other words, some souls complete their purpose quickly, while others still have work to do, and return. This notion of soul contracts – that our time on Earth is predetermined, guided by lessons we need to learn – echoes throughout many spiritual traditions. As Monica Berg also explained, some souls fulfil their purpose in a short time, while others return for longer journeys of learning and transformation: "It's not about how long we live, but how fully we live."

Marielle's words about soul contracts resonated deeply, though their full meaning wouldn't become clear until I experienced my own first pregnancy loss. I lay on the ultrasound bed, desperately hoping that the consultants were wrong and my four-and-a-half-month-old foetus was actually healthy. I'd read stories online about misdiagnoses and clung to each one with every fibre of my being, praying that my experience was a mistake. Then, my worst fears were confirmed: my precious baby would most likely not survive outside the womb. I looked at my partner and burst into tears. Though I'd cried for days after first being told, I hadn't let myself fully believe it until now. In that unbearable moment, I thought of the words of Monica and Marielle: some souls complete their sacred contract in only a short time. It didn't erase my grief, but it gave me a different way to hold it. I knew what had to happen, and the days that followed remain a blur. The only light in this heartbreak was the profound gifts this soul had brought me in such a short time. Of course, I grieved. But I was also filled with gratitude. I had been given a renewed sense of faith, a deepened love for my partner, and the knowledge that I wasn't infertile, despite what I'd been told years before. Deep within, I knew this wasn't an ending. It was simply a pause. I knew I would be reunited with this angel who had changed my life so profoundly. I held a sacred ritual for my unborn son and thanked him for the gifts he had brought me: love, perspective and a deeper connection to the divine.

Echoes of the past

The belief that death isn't the end is often linked to the idea of reincarnation, which describes the continuity of the soul across lifetimes. Ancient philosophical texts foundational to Hinduism, Jainism, Buddhism, Celtic mythology and Western mystical traditions all draw on this wisdom.

In 1966, with the publication of his book, *Twenty Cases Suggestive of Reincarnation*, Professor Ian Stevenson shifted the conversation around reincarnation from religious contexts into mainstream culture. He spent over 40 years investigating accounts of reincarnation, primarily from children, to find evidence of its validity. He observed that, around the age of three, some children often began sharing vivid, specific memories from what seemed like a different life. Some would say, "When I was big, I used to have blue eyes", or recall working in a particular job or living in another town. Some children even mentioned events from before they were born, stating, "That happened before I was in mummy's tummy." One of the most striking aspects of these cases was the detailed nature of the children's memories. Some spoke of spouses, or described how they had died, recounting accidents or traumatic events like, "I died in a car accident." In many cases, the memories began to fade as the children grew older, usually around age seven. However, before that time, these children were able to describe verifiable information, both about people who had died and other events. Even more astonishing were cases where children bore birthmarks or physical defects that matched injuries or wounds of the person they claimed to have been.

Among the many extraordinary cases Stevenson investigated, one stands out for its depth and documentation: that of Shanti Devi, a young girl who grew up in 1930s

India. At a very young age, Shanti began sharing detailed memories of a past life as a woman named Lugdi Devi, who had lived in a nearby town. She spoke in a detailed way about everything from Lugdi's former husband to the layout of their home. When Stevenson meticulously researched Shanti's claims, he found they corresponded with the real life of Lugdi Devi. Astonishingly, Shanti was able to recognise her former husband and family members when she met them, despite never having visited their town or known them in this life. She even spoke the dialect of Lugdi's town, a language she had never been exposed to before. The emotional depth of her memories, and her expressions of love for her former husband, further deepened the complexity and authenticity of this remarkable case.

Another compelling example is the case of James Leininger, a young boy from Louisiana who at the age of two began experiencing vivid nightmares of a plane crash. He recounted specific details of the incident, including the type of plane, the name of the ship it took off from, and the names of his fellow pilots. These details were later verified to align with the experiences of a World-War-II pilot named James Huston Jr., who had died decades earlier. Little James also began sharing specific family details, like nicknames, and anecdotes about his former father. When researchers tracked down Big James' surviving sister, she confirmed his statements were accurate.

Whether you believe these accounts or not, opening yourself to the possibility of reincarnation can bring a deep sense of interconnectedness. After all, there's no evidence to suggest reincarnation doesn't happen. Embracing this possibility encourages us to live with greater empathy for those in different circumstances – not just for this life, but for all the lives to come.

Along my journey, I've encountered many remarkable

stories of past lives. One such example presented itself to me in 2009, during a trip to Thailand. A friend of a friend connected me with someone who lived in Bangkok, and so when I arrived in the city, we arranged to meet. Little did I know that our conversation would have a lasting impact on my life. Our lunch turned into an afternoon, and, towards the end, she opened up about her son. Years before, he had experienced problems teething. It had been extremely traumatic and painful. Every night, he would wake and gnaw at his mouth, causing his gums to bleed. For nights on end, the mother would rush into his room on hearing him cry and find the little boy in agony. She took him to every doctor she could find, but no one was able to help. She even flew him to different countries in the hope that other medical systems might offer a solution, but she had no success. After months of worry, a friend suggested she speak to an astrologer and spiritual healer. I listened as the elegant woman in front of me explained that she had little faith in this practitioner. She had been brought up to be so scientifically minded that the idea that an astrologist could help felt almost laughable. But she had nothing to lose.

During the short call, the astrologist said, "I would like you to buy a small fridge, fill it with food, and place it in his bedroom. Before he goes to sleep, I want you to show your son that the fridge is full of food." This was confusing. She knew her child wasn't hungry; how would a small fridge help the matter? Nevertheless, she did as she was told. From that moment on, her son never gnawed his gums again. "What happened?" I asked in disbelief. "Why did he stop? What did the astrologist do?" She had called the astrologer the very next morning to ask the same question. The astrologer knew she was close-minded, so at first she urged her just to count her blessings and move on. But my new friend was determined

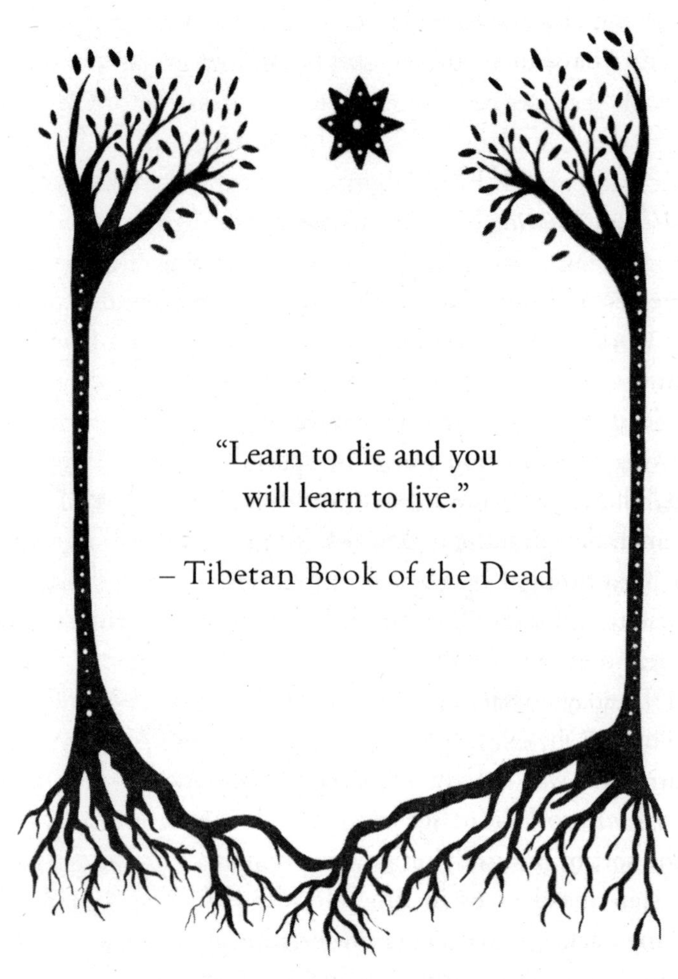

"Learn to die and you
will learn to live."

– Tibetan Book of the Dead

to know. The astrologer finally shared that in a past life, her son had been a starving refugee who had died at an early age. He was trapped dreaming about this recent lifetime, and too young to realise this wasn't his life anymore. The food helped him, on a deep soul level, realise that life was different: he didn't have to go hungry anymore, and he could release the fear.

Death's wisdom

There seems to be a common understanding among those who work with the dying that people know when the end is near.

"Several of them even cooked meals to leave in the freezer, knowing that the food would come in handy once they had died," shares Felicity Warner, the founder of Soul Midwives.[84] "I remember speaking to one lady and she asked, 'When will your next hospital visit be?' And I replied, 'Well, it'll be next Thursday and then I'll come and see you.' And she said, 'Oh no, no, don't worry about that, my dear. I'm going to die next Tuesday afternoon when *Neighbours* is on.' I remember thinking, 'Oh, okay, how extraordinary.' And do you know what? That was exactly what happened – she died during *Neighbours*, so I didn't see her again. This is so characteristic of the sort of things dying people often say. It's as if they are one step ahead of us in time already, and they are already looking back. I find that very interesting in terms of how we can understand the nature of consciousness."

In the end death is simply a change of address. We move on, and the energy we've created in this life continues with us. What we do today shapes not only this lifetime, but also the ones to come. The law of cause and effect is always present;

how we choose to live is inevitably reflected back to us, for better or worse. Ask yourself this:

> How do you wish to live, knowing that what you do will echo into the future?

> How do you wish to live, knowing that death is simply another step in your soul's eternal journey?

The idea of soul groups – clusters of souls who travel together through many lifetimes – shows up not only in ancient mystical traditions but also in modern clinical research. Psychologist and hypnotherapist Michael Newton,[85] through thousands of hypnotherapy sessions, found people describing almost identical experiences: soul groups of about ten to 25 members who reincarnate together in different roles – as family, friends, mentors or even challengers – to help one another grow.

Newton discovered these stories through regression therapy, where hypnosis or deep relaxation helps people access memories buried in the subconscious, sometimes from childhood, and sometimes, as they describe, from past lives. Similarly, Dr Elisabeth Kübler-Ross, famous for her research on death and dying, noticed that many of her patients reported being "greeted" by familiar presences as they moved closer to death, a finding she believed hinted at ongoing soul connections beyond this life.[86] Together, their observations suggest that the idea of soul groups isn't just spiritual poetry; it might reflect a universal human experience, spanning clinical observation, anecdotal research and spiritual history.

However, even knowing that we most likely will see our treasured loved ones in the next realm, this does not stop us from missing them now. Dr Christina Oakley-Harrington, founder of London's renowned occult bookshop Treadwell's and a respected scholar of Western esotericism, believes her magical rituals have transformed her relationship with grief. "I've experienced a lot of loss in my life. My parents, my friends, even my dog, who was like my child. But I grieve freely. I'm not embarrassed by my grief. The rituals I've practised over the years have given me space to embrace death. Every autumn, we hold ceremonies to remember those who've passed. It's taught me that sadness isn't something to shy away from; it's part of the human experience." Creating time to honour grief and open communication with those who've passed over further heals our relationship and understanding with death.

To truly embrace life, we must also embrace death. What will make you proud at the end of this journey? And how can you live today with this in mind? Each challenge, each loss, is an opportunity to be born again into a new version of yourself, to appreciate the gift of life, and connect even further to the greater mysteries of existence.

The law of conservation of energy means that energy can't be made or eliminated; it only changes form. Mother Nature reflects this truth everywhere: the energy of what dies becomes nourishment for new life, part of the endless cycle that connects and sustains everything. This wisdom of nature is where we turn next.

The Moon card reminds us that nature is an endless source of wisdom, always ready to guide us. Just as the moon waxes and wanes, showing only part of its face at any given time, so too does life reveal itself in fragments. To live magically is to stay attuned to these rhythms, remain connected to nature, and to honour Mother Earth for sustaining all life.

Reconnect with Mother Nature

"Wash yourself in the pure water of the streams, put your bare feet on the good earth, and fall asleep in the arms of an ancient tree. There is good medicine to be found in nature … it heals the soul."

– Rosemary Gladstar

For over a decade, I rejected my countryside upbringing for the bright lights of the city and matrix ideals. I was dazzled by late-night parties and early morning meetings in heels and coordinated outfits, believing this was the road to productivity and "fortune". I'd forgotten what the warm embrace of nature felt like, so I no longer looked for it. It was only through this journey of exploring the forgotten wisdom of witches, taking inspiration from so many deeply grounded thinkers and healers, that I realised how much I was missing. I had barely noticed the trees that lined the roads of my daily commute, nor had I spotted the daffodils arriving in spring. Like reuniting with an old friend, I needed to re-meet Mother Nature. Witnessing the magic of nature is like touching the divine. Whether it's the vastness of the ocean, the quiet strength of mountains, or the whispering breeze on a warm evening, these moments are healing. Reconnecting with nature is about inviting Earth's intelligence back into your body and soul.

Our ancestors' relationship with Earth was holy; they considered themselves children of the Earth and honoured her unconditional giving. But today, this couldn't be more different. Since 1800, nature-based terms have declined by 60 per cent.[87] The language of birds, and wildflowers has slipped from our speech, and with them, our connection to the living world. A UK study reveals that 83 per cent of children can't identify a bumblebee,[88] and nearly half don't recognise a bluebell. In 2007, the *Oxford Junior Dictionary* removed even more entries related to the natural world, including "acorn" and "magpie", to make room for modern inventions like "blog" and "MP3 player". There were protests to stop this, but the dictionary doesn't include what we'd ideally like; it's a factual reflection of how we speak. We've swapped sunsets for screens and we search for cures in sterile labs. We are on the brink of losing sight of the wisdom under our feet.

How nature heals you biochemically

"When was the last time you spent time in nature?" an elderly witch asked me a few years ago. I was blank. I had been consumed by work for years and had barely even visited my parents' home in the countryside. "Find her again and appreciate her," she said softly. Not long after that conversation, an unexpected work opportunity arose, one that would take me to the Red Sea in Saudi Arabia. At a time when I was struggling with extreme anxiety, I took the opportunity to swim each morning in the ocean, near the hotel. After a few days,

I felt mysteriously calmer, as if the ocean itself was dissolving my anxiety.

It wasn't until later that I learned why this happened: the sea wasn't just soothing me emotionally, it was healing me on a cellular level. Sea air is charged with negative ions, tiny particles created when waves crash against the shore that are shown to boost serotonin levels, which lifts mood and restores calm. The rhythm of the waves also pulses at around 0.2 Hz, the same frequency as our optimal breath rate (5–6 breaths a minute) for nervous-system regulation and deep meditation. This is why, without even thinking, we naturally slow our breathing, inhale more deeply, and feel ourselves softening in the presence of the sea. No wonder they call it "vitamin sea".

Since ancient times, witches have known and revered the healing power of the ocean. In Mesopotamia, the god of the ocean, Enki, was associated with wisdom, magic, art, healing and fertility. Today, science confirms these early instincts about the sea's power, with researchers at Exeter University observing that people living near the sea are 22 per cent less likely to suffer from mental health issues than those further inland.[89]

Natural environments calm overstimulated minds in ways that human-made surroundings cannot. Unlike the sharp angles of urban life, nature's soft, wonky forms relax our gaze and let our thoughts wander. We evolved without straight lines so it is only relatively recently that our eyes had to adapt to the angular urban landscape. The technical term for this is "attention restoration theory". When we narrowly direct our attention on sharp edges like mindlessly scrolling on phones or staring at laptop screens, it's visually distressing compared to what we're used to. "Undirected attention", however, where our eyes and minds are free to wander natural landscapes, creates a sense of familiarity and calm.[90] When we swap screens for scenery, our minds and biochemistry have a chance to reset.

From Mother Sea to Mother Forest, nature wraps us in her arms if we let her. Like a parental embrace, nature restores us because she is the one who's shaped us for millions of years. Our bodies recognise her signals. Biologist Edward O. Wilson called this *biophilia* – our deep, biological longing to return to the wild world we came from. "We breathe air exhaled from trees whose leaves are made of starlight. Our veins echo the patterns of rivers, branches, and root systems. We aren't a part of nature. We are nature", writes Marysia Miernowska, further capturing our unique relationship.

Easy ways to reconnect with Nature: grounding

With most of us living in towns and cities, reconnecting with nature can feel difficult. Thankfully, there are many ways to benefit from Mother Earth's energetic gifts without making a dramatic pilgrimage to faraway lands (though this is a great option, of course). Nature is everywhere if you look closely. Try:

- Taking off your shoes in the garden or park
- Sitting under a tree or lying on the grass
- Noticing which plants grow wild in your area
- Listening for birdsong, or watching cloud shapes drift.

The Earth's surface carries a gentle negative charge, rich in healing electrons. When you walk barefoot on the soil your body absorbs negative ions, a process called grounding. Even small moments of connection like this can reawaken your bond with the Earth.

> Ask yourself:
>
> • What grows here without tending? What catches
>   my attention?
>
> Start where you are. Magic lives there too.

The wood wide web

Historically, witches lived on the edge of woods, and for good reason. Forests are alive with medicine. Trees release phytoncides, natural antimicrobial compounds that not only strengthen our immune defences but also lower stress hormones like cortisol. In Japan, researchers have found that spending just three days in a forest significantly improves the immune system and the benefits last for more than a month.[91] Even when we can't step outside, simply gazing at trees through a window has been shown to speed up healing. In one study, patients with a view of nature healed faster, required less pain medication, and reported feeling more at ease than those staring at a blank brick wall.[92] The witches have always known what science is finally catching up to. Forests might be without Wi-Fi, but you're likely to find a better connection.

Trees are far more like us than we might imagine. They form deep familial bonds, caring for one another through the "wood wide web" – a vast underground network of fungal threads. Fungi are their telephone lines and internet connection. They carry whispered messages between trees and weave together entire ecosystems in a silent choreography of collaboration. Like human families, through this network trees shelter their young, feed struggling neighbours, and even keep dying elders alive for decades. As Merlin Sheldrake writes, "intelligence is not limited to brains."[93] The intelligence of these fungi systems shaped the planet's destiny, making life on land possible. They remind us that survival is far from a solitary pursuit, but a shared rhythm, one rooted in reciprocity and the deep intelligence of connection.

I gained firsthand insight into the sentient nature of trees during a trip to my parents' home in the countryside. There's a cherished wood nearby, a haven of tranquillity for thousands of locals. Its future was uncertain, threatened by plans for a high-speed rail line that would decimate half of its ancient woodland. A group of activists had set up a protest camp within the woods, determined to prevent the destruction. Despite their tireless efforts, the plans moved forwards. Capitalistic short-sightedness was trumping common sense and community spirit. With the wood's fate sealed, my mother and I wandered through the bluebell-carpeted trails, our hearts heavy with the knowledge that many of her beloved trees were marked for felling. I returned to London that evening feeling sad about the impending fate of the forest.

The next day my mother called with an astonishing tale. On her very last morning walk before the cutting began, she found one of the marked trees had seemingly fallen of its own accord. There had been no storm or wind, yet a giant tree had inexplicably fallen across the path. Although this sounds farfetched, it really does appear like a tree had taken its own life in protest, just hours before the workers had their way. There was no evidence of human intervention. Instead, the tree just happened to have 'fallen' from its roots the day before it was supposed to go. Maybe the wood wide web had warned this ancient wisdom-keeper of what was to come and, in defiance, he wanted to fall first on his own terms.

Lessons from nature: wild wisdom

Nature is the greatest spiritual teacher. Across every species, season and survival strategy, it offers profound truths about how to live, grow and adapt.

Phenomenon	Lesson
Nature uses energy to navigate → Bees navigate using magnetic fields to find their way – even on cloudy days.	• Bees don't rely on logic alone, they trust energy and unseen forces to guide them. So should we.
Every role is sacred → Every bee has a role, be it as a worker, drone or queen. Each holds equal importance.	• Purpose isn't about prestige. Your contribution, however quiet, matters deeply.
Work hard, rest fully → Bees sleep 5–8 hours a day, often curled up with others.	• Even the busiest beings need restoration. Rest isn't laziness – it's wisdom.
Slowness can be a power → Sloths move so slowly that algae grows on them, camouflaging them in the forest.	• Slowness can be a superpower. Life doesn't always reward the fastest – it honours harmony.
Turn towards the light → Sunflowers follow the sun throughout the day.	• Follow what warms you. Where your attention goes, your energy grows.
Adaptability is intelligence → Octopuses change colour and texture instantly to blend into their surroundings.	• Sometimes survival means being fluid, not fixed. Adaptation is magic.
Desire fuels evolution → Giraffes evolved long necks to reach higher food sources.	• When your needs stretch beyond your environment, growth follows.
Beauty can bloom from mud → The lotus flower grows from murky, stagnant waters.	• Challenge doesn't block your bloom – it prepares you for it. Darkness is fertile.
Shedding what no longer serves → Snakes regularly shed their skin to grow.	• Release is natural. Growth requires letting go of what you've outgrown.

Phenomenon	Lesson
Joy is a signal → Parrots dance to attract mates, often bobbing and grooving to rhythms.	• Joy magnetises. Your delight might be your most powerful attractor.
Nature thrives in symbiosis → Bees and flowers evolved together in a process of mutual adaptation.	• You're part of a greater system. Collaboration – not competition – sustains life.
Transformation requires surrender → Caterpillars dissolve into goo before emerging as butterflies.	• The biggest transformations often look like falling apart. Trust the mess – it's alchemy.
Love is shared in small acts → Penguins huddle for warmth, sharing body heat in brutal cold.	• Connection sustains us. Tiny gestures of care can protect entire communities.

Plants are our allies

We need nature. Nature doesn't need us. If the plants vanished, so would we. However, if humans were to disappear tomorrow, nature would flourish. Herbalism is more than a healing practice, it's a powerful reminder of our dependence on the Earth. Every breath we take, every meal we eat, every cell in our body owes its life to the intelligence of the natural world. Without nature's gifts, we would've perished long ago.

Herbalism is as old as humanity itself, woven into the roots of our survival. Archaeologists have uncovered evidence of herbal knowledge in our earliest ancestors: Neanderthals used yarrow and chamomile over 60,000 years ago, and Ötzi the Iceman – frozen in the Alps for over 5,000 years – was found carrying a pouch of healing herbs and fungi.

For millennia, herbalists were trusted guides, caretakers of plant wisdom. But their reverence for nature eventually put them at odds with Church dogma. They called it witchcraft when women healed with herbs, but science when men put it in a pill. Thousands were persecuted, not for harming, but for healing. Their crime? Sharing the Earth's wisdom.

The rainforest apothecary

A few years ago, I was trekking through the Amazon in search of one of the oldest trees. My guide turned to me and said, "Everything we need for a healthy life is right here; this forest is my pharmacy." Pointing to the bark of a cinchona tree, he explained, "This is the cure for malaria." His words revealed an important truth: while science continues to advance, the core of our healing is – and always has been – thanks to nature. And yet, natural remedies are too often dismissed as "primitive" or "placebo", even though they form the foundation of modern medicine. Nearly 40 per cent of pharmaceutical drugs are derived from plants.[94] The aspirin that soothes your headaches comes from the bark of the white willow tree. Digoxin, crucial for treating heart failure, is sourced from foxglove. Taxol, a chemotherapy drug for cancer, is found in the Pacific yew tree. Morphine, a potent pain-reliever, originates from the opium poppy. And yet, humanity keeps destroying the hand that protects its health.

Flower power

Flowers hold more power than we often realise. Far from being just pretty, they have energetic properties that can restore balance in subtle and profound ways. The idea of using flower essences for healing re-emerged in the 12th century, when a German mystic named Hildegard of Bingen began writing about the spiritual and energetic qualities of plants. After experiencing visions, she believed that each flower carried its own unique healing signature – an energetic code or "greening power" that could support emotional and spiritual well-being.

Centuries later, in the early 20th century, Dr. Edward Bach, a British physician, picked up this thread. Frustrated by conventional medicine's narrow focus on treating physical symptoms, he began researching plants that could support emotional healing. His work led to the creation of the now-famous Bach Flower Remedies, 38 flower-based essences designed to help restore inner harmony.

He saw that physical ailments were manifestations of emotional and psychological dis-ease, and so the magic of flower essences lies not just in their chemistry, but in their character. Watch how a flower grows, and you'll learn what it offers on a deeper level.

Flower first aid

Below are examples of different essences and the challenges they support.

Flower Essence	Emotion or Challenge	Energetic Support	How It Grows / What It Teaches
White Chestnut	Repetitive thoughts, mental loops	Restores mental clarity and peace	Grows upright and steady, like focused thought; teaches stillness amid mental clutter.
Mimulus	Fear of known things (e.g., public speaking, flying)	Encourages bravery to face fears	A delicate wildflower that thrives near water; teaches quiet courage and adaptability.

Flower Essence	Emotion or Challenge	Energetic Support	How It Grows / What It Teaches
Larch	Lack of confidence, fear of failure	Builds self-worth and inner confidence	A tall, resilient tree that sheds and renews, reminds us that growth comes through cycles, not perfection.
Wild Oat	Feeling lost or uncertain about direction	Clarifies purpose and soul direction	Spreads freely across open fields; shows the value of exploration before clarity.
Elm	Temporary overwhelm from responsibility	Restores inner strength and balance	A broad, sheltering tree; symbolises grounded leadership and support without collapse.
Star of Bethlehem	Grief, shock, emotional trauma	Comforts and heals deep emotional wounds	Blooms even after disturbance; teaches restoration after heartbreak.
Impatiens	Impatience, irritability	Promotes patience and acceptance	Grows quickly and bursts its seeds; a reminder to slow down and trust divine timing.
Clematis	Disconnection, daydreaming, escapism	Anchors presence in the here and now	Climbs and entwines; shows how imagination can root into the present to create beauty.
Crab Apple	Feeling unclean, self-disgust, fixation on flaws	Cleanses and soothes inner self-judgement	Blooms in pure white clusters; a symbol of self-purification and renewal.

Whether it's soothing a nettle sting with dock leaves, sipping chamomile tea, massaging rose oil into tired hands, or burning herbs to cleanse a space, these practices reconnect us with the Earth's rhythms. As the legendary Rosemary Gladstar writes, "brewed with intent and a bit of 'kitchen magic', herbal tea offers more than meets the eye. Along with herbs and water, there's also earth, sky, sunlight and stars captured in this cup."

When you open your eyes to the magic of plants, everything changes. Each plant has its own unique personality. Next time you go on a walk, notice which plants or flowers catch your eye: do you know their names? The ancient practice of herbalism is a journey that continues to provide more gifts. With 374,000 known plant species, we've barely scratched the surface of their potential.

Reconnecting with your inner herbalist

One of the simple ways to start your journey into magical herbalism is by making your own flower essence. These vibrational remedies, created by infusing a flower into water, often under sunlight or moonlight, harness the subtle energy of plants. To create your own, you'll need:

- Fresh, blooming flowers
- A glass or crystal bowl
- Pure, filtered water
- A sunny or moonlit location
- A brown glass bottle with a dropper
- Brandy/vodka/apple cider vinegar for preservation
- A smaller bottle for dilution (optional)

Process:
1. Choose your flower: Ideally a flower that resonates with you or addresses a specific emotional need.[95]
2. Prepare your space: Find a sunny, quiet location to create your essence.
3. Harvest your flowers: Gently pick the blossoms, ensuring they are fresh and vibrant.

4. Infuse in water: Place the flowers in a glass bowl filled with pure water and expose it to direct sunlight or moonlight for several hours.
5. Preserve the essence: Strain the water into a brown[96] glass bottle, adding an equal amount of alcohol as a preservative.

Important considerations:

- Intention: Crucial for any work with herb magic. Focus your mind on your goal.
- Timing: Choose a sunny day or a clear moonlit night for optimal energy transfer.
- Preservation: While brandy is a traditional preservative, you can also explore alternatives such as apple cider vinegar.
- Testing: Experiment with different flowers and amounts to find what works best for you.
- Flower essences should not replace conventional medicine. Always consult a healthcare professional if you have significant health concerns.

To continue on your herbal journey, here are some of my favourite ingredients to work with magically:

Rose

The rose, often hailed as the queen of flowers, has served as a sacred symbol of beauty, love and devotion throughout history. It was cherished by ancient Egyptians, who used roses in perfumes and embalming rituals, associating the flower with their exalted goddess, Isis. Cleopatra, one of the first great witches, was said to have bathed in pure rosewater, enhancing her beauty and power. According to another tale, a

Persian princess would fill the royal fountains with rosewater so that anyone walking through the garden would be sprinkled with healing drops.

The significance of the rose extends beyond its pretty petals. Its vibrational energy emits a frequency of 320 MHz, the highest among plants, making it a tangible representation of love. This unique frequency is said to open the energetic centre in the chest (the heart chakra), enhancing romance while magnifying allure and attraction. Additionally, the geraniol and citronellol compounds in roses have calming and antiseptic effects.

You can harness the nurturing qualities of roses through various forms, such as rose petals, oils and teas. The rose instils a calm, confident energy that harmonises the heart's rhythms. This flower touches the spiritual heart in a way few others can, helping individuals to find love within themselves and extend it outwards. Connected to the divine feminine, the rose is particularly beneficial for women experiencing hormonal and fertility imbalances, as well as for men seeking to reconnect with their inner feminine power. If you're not growing your own, and to fully benefit from the rose's healing properties, it's crucial to source organically grown varieties from the *Rosa* genus. Most commercially available roses are treated with harmful pesticides, which detract from their natural powers.

Uses for rose:

- Nourishing fertility: Pair with goji berries – thought to improve circulation and support both male and female reproductive health.
- Supporting healthy libido: Combine with cacao and cinnamon.

- Harmonising the menstrual cycle: Combine with vitex berry.

Lavender

Lavender has shaped my life. My parents live on a lavender farm, so lavender reminds me of maternal and paternal love. My mother uses lavender everywhere: in the bathroom, in shortbread and even in cordial for cocktails. Lavender has long been considered a kind of magic potion, as the ancient Egyptians and Greeks well understood. The Egyptians used it in mummification rituals for its antiseptic and preservative properties, while the Greeks and Romans infused it into bathwater for its calming and cleansing effects. Its Latin name *lavare*, meaning "to wash", reflects its ancient use as a natural cleanser.

And lavender truly is medicine. If you cut yourself, you can turn to this purple friend. It contains powerful compounds, linalool and camphor, that have antimicrobial properties. These compounds disrupt the membranes of bacteria, fungi, and viruses, protecting the body and speeding healing. One of my favourite everyday potions is lavender hydrosol, also called lavender water, a byproduct of lavender oil distillation. It gently clears spots on your skin thanks to its natural antibacterial and anti-inflammatory compounds, while also working as a surface cleanser in the kitchen. It soothes and sanitises, and smells divine, whether you're tending to your face or wiping down your chopping board. A floral forcefield, in every sense. If you step into my mother's kitchen, you will be hit with a wonderful wave of lavender.

Herbalist Rosemary Gladstar calls lavender a "mild antidepressant", helpful for lifting depression and melancholy. It's also one of nature's best sleep aids. Key compounds within, like linalyl acetate, interact with GABA receptors in the brain, those responsible for calming the nervous system, helping to slow heart rate, ease brain activity, and gently prepare the body for rest. Lavender is not just a flower, it's a comforter, a protector, and a quiet alchemist of calm.

Tips for working with lavender:

- Put 3-4 drops of lavender oil into the bath at night for better sleep.
- Use lavender hydrosol as a natural cleaner and facial toner.
- For a minor cut or wound, never apply undiluted lavender oil directly, but mix a few drops of lavender essential oil with a carrier oil like coconut or olive oil.
- Apply once mixed.

Cacao

When I was in New York, I was invited to my first cacao ceremony, which is a meditation supported by the cacao drink, organised by a practicioner from Guatemala. It was a full moon. We sat in a circle and were given a cup of very dark brown liquid. I had little knowledge of cacao and naïvely assumed it would be like Cadbury's hot chocolate. I was wrong. What we understand as chocolate today is quite different from ceremonial cacao. Unlike processed chocolate, which has often been so diluted that it contains more cream and sugar than cocoa, ceremonial cacao is rich in antioxidants, vitamins and minerals. Its strength and purity give cacao its spiritual nature and its ability to enhance intuition and open the heart. I also double-checked that this was not going to make me hallucinate as I hadn't signed up for that on a Monday evening.

The taste was strong and bitter. It was remarkably calming, and I quickly started to enjoy the strength. Once we had all finished our cups, we were invited to close our eyes and connect with the spirit of the cacao. My meditation felt far deeper than usual as I drifted into a calm altered state of consciousness. An overwhelming sense of peace and harmony swept over me.

You can trace the magic of cacao back to the Olmec civilisation around 1500BCE. The cacao tree, *Theobroma cacao*, was considered divine, described as the "food of the gods" and "heart blood", and revered for its medicinal and metaphysical properties. These include the relaxing theobromine, which dilates the cardiovascular system; mood-enhancing compounds like serotonin and anandamide (often referred to as the "bliss molecule"); and phenylethylamine, also known as the love chemical, as it is also released when falling in love. We can also thank the love chemical for cacao's aphrodisiac benefits.

In ancient Mexico, cacao beans were once valued more highly than gold and used as a currency. When the Spanish arrived in the Americas, they encountered this exotic ceremonial drink, and it was then that the medicinal benefits of cacao began to spread globally. A Spanish army surgeon in 1796 was quoted saying, "Chocolate is a divine, celestial drink, the sweat of the stars, the vital seed, divine nectar, the drink of the gods, panacea and universal medicine." Thousands of years on from those first sacred ceremonies, cacao is still used as a powerful way to connect with the Earth's energy and the gentle, nurturing quality often referred to as the spirit of Mama Cacao. While you can prepare your own cacao elixir, I recommend exploring a local cacao ceremony if one is available to you, to experience its depth and intention within a shared, guided setting.

Nature is always in motion, renewing, recalibrating, and offering her wisdom to those who pay attention. When we move in rhythm with her cycles, we begin to see ourselves more clearly. Whether it's in the quiet community of a forest, the vastness of the ocean, or the steady turning of the moon, her patterns remind us how to live. As one of my favourite authors, Sharon Blackie, writes, "It's a contract you see, people and the land. You care for it, and it cares for you".[97]

Nature shows us that nothing exists in isolation. When a forest falls in one place, the air changes in another. Cause and effect are not abstract principles but living truths that nature demonstrates daily. We are not separate nations, but threads woven into the same delicate web of life.

That same web, the invisible current binding all things, is the foundation of how magic works. Every spell and ritual is simply an act of conscious participation in this living conversation between self and universe. This is the path we follow next.

The Magician is the archetype of manifestation and magical agency, which is the ability to turn ideas into reality. With one hand pointing to the sky, and the other to the earth, he signifies the channelling of divine energy into material form. The Magician reminds us that rituals are how we focus energy, and spells are how we speak the unseen into form.

Activate your magic with rituals and spells

"A ritual isn't magic because it changes the world. It's magic because it changes us."

– Martha Beck

Magic is the art of inner transformation. When you change your inner landscape, your outer world rearranges itself to match. Rituals and spells are the practical tools that help you do exactly that.

We are all spellcasters, whether we realise it or not. Every thought, emotion and action sends ripples of energy into the universe, shaping what we experience. Drift through life without intention, and you may find yourself creating a future you never wanted. But it doesn't have to be this way.

Habits can be dangerous because they are actions that have become so familiar that we participate in them without thinking. It may be efficient to make a cup of tea while thinking about something else, but it steals away magical potential.

When you turn habits into rituals – conscious acts infused with meaning – you reclaim your power to shape your life. They elevate the ordinary into the sacred, connecting you to the divine, a portal of power. Rituals bridge the physical with the spiritual, turning mundane moments into tools for manifestation.

Rituals don't need to be big or complex; what truly matters is the meaning we bring to them. Your morning coffee can either be a rushed nuisance or a grounding moment asking for what you need. For example, as you stir, and sip, you could whisper, *please bring me peace and inspiration today*. Your morning commute can be a stressful journey or a chance to read uplifting books, setting your vibe for the day ahead. Each ritual becomes a small act of devotion, aligning you with the energy you want to carry into the day or night.

Modern research confirms that rituals biologically change us. In one study, 75 Hindu women in Mauritius were asked to prepare and deliver a public speech, which the researchers knew would trigger anxiety. Half of the group was asked to perform temple rituals in preparation, while the other half was told simply to rest. Despite similar anxiety levels at the start, those who engaged in ritual reported significantly lower stress levels, a result confirmed by their heart-rate data.[98] Over 30 trillion cells in your body eavesdrop on your thoughts,[99] so rituals can not only programme your psyche but your entire being, aligning thought, energy and action. The impact of ritual is overwhelmingly overlooked.

Psychologists call this the *ritual effect*: the brain perceives structure and intention as soothing, slowing anxious patterns of thought. MRI scans show that during intentional acts, the regions linked to planning and emotional regulation light up. In this way, rituals work like an emotional remote control, helping you change the channel when life gets noisy.

Understanding the "why" behind your ritual amplifies the impact. Rafael Nadal, one of the best tennis players of all time, has his own magical ritual for inviting success, namely in using energy gel before he plays. He rips off the top, folds the side over and squeezes four times. He never squeezes two or five times, only four. But why? Nadal once explained how this has a tangible effect on his mind, "It's something I don't need to do, but when I do it, it means I'm focused."[100] Deliberate actions create deliberate intentions. They help you step into a more empowered state of mind.

In relationships, rituals create a unique energy between people. This holds true whether it's a regular date night with a partner, a special handshake with a friend, or the routine scrambled eggs on a Saturday morning with someone you love. The co-founder of Netflix, Marc Randolf, credits a simple ritual, his Tuesday date night with his wife, for keeping him balanced while building one of the world's most recognisable media brands. He shared this reflection, "For over 30 years, I had a hard cut-off on Tuesdays. Rain or shine, I left at exactly 5pm to spend the evening with my best friend. Whether we went to a movie, had dinner, or just window-shopped, nothing got in the way – no meeting, no last-minute request. Those Tuesday nights kept me sane and put the rest of my work in perspective. I resolved early on not to become one of those entrepreneurs on their seventh startup and seventh wife. What I'm most proud of isn't the companies I've built; it's staying married to the same woman, watching my kids grow up knowing me, and having time to pursue my passions. That's my definition of success."[101] Rituals are beautiful, they can be so small and yet they help us affirm and reinforce our values.

Rituals for alchemising your inner world

Rituals for emotional release, such as water cleansing or breath-work, are simple yet powerful ways to process emotion and let go of what we no longer need. They work like emotional hygiene, keeping our hearts clear and our energy light.

Water ritual

We know that water is a potent symbol of purification, so why not turn your shower into a magical ritual? As the water flows over you, visualise it as a purifying force that washes away any tension, fear or stuck frustration. While doing this, speak the words:

> With this water, release all energy that is not mine or is no longer serving me. Any tension, worries or fear can be let go.

As you watch the water run down the drain, imagine it carrying away your worries, leaving you feeling refreshed and renewed.

Breath ritual

By focusing on your breath, you can clear away stuck energy and enter a calmer, more centred state at any moment. Begin by inhaling deeply through your nose, holding your breath for a count of four, then exhaling slowly through your mouth for seven. Repeat this process at least ten times, allowing yourself to focus on each breath. As you breathe, visualise every exhale as taking away anything you don't want and every inhale as a drawing in of peace and balance. To deepen the practice, say to yourself:

> I breathe in peace, I release tension.

You can experiment with different visualisations for what each inhalation and exhalation represents. Perhaps your inhalation draws in white light, healing energy to nourish specific areas of the body, while your exhalation pushes out toxic influences from your personal space.

Rituals for self-discovery and unblocking creativity

Morning pages

One of the most powerful rituals for calming busy minds, processing worries, and unlocking creativity is the practice of morning pages. Introduced by Julia Cameron in 1992 in her best-selling book *The Artist's Way*, this simple ritual involves writing three pages every morning of free-flowing thoughts. It's a process that takes about 20 minutes but can transform your entire life. This is not an exaggeration. If you can commit to this ritual, you will be tremendously rewarded with wisdom, peace and discernment.

During my interview with Julia, she described the effect of morning pages, saying: "What I find with morning pages is that it's a little bit like taking a tiny little broom, sticking it into all the corners of your life and bringing the rubble and debris to the centre of the room where you can deal with it. So when you write morning pages, you're saying to the universe, this is what I like. This is what I don't like. This is what I want more of. This is what I want less of. It brings you honesty, authenticity, and vulnerability." She continued, "Morning pages help you to expand. What happens is they will bring up a risk and you'll say, I can't do that. And then they'll bring up the risk again and you'll think, I don't think I can do that. And then finally, just to hush them up when they say it again, you say, oh, all right, I'll try. Unless you take that initial risk, you cannot succeed or expand."

While the first few days may feel easy, the ritual soon becomes more challenging as the obvious thoughts are exhausted. But this is where the magic begins. Your hand seems to take over, and a conversation with your subconscious mind begins to unfold. Through this process, thoughts, feelings and ideas rise from the depths of your being, often surprising you with their unexpected wisdom.

As Julia says, "Morning pages are a spiritual practice, not a writing practice. They are about anything and everything that crosses your mind – and they are for your eyes only." Even if you start with just journalling for one page, this ritual is by far the most effective way to change how you feel about difficult emotions and become unstuck. I've personally found more transformation in morning pages than in meditation. Through writing, you naturally connect with both your subconscious and superconscious mind. I'm excited for you to experience their power, when solutions begin to surface with surprising ease and clarity.

Gratitude ritual

Gratitude rituals unlock the fullness of life. It turns what we have into enough, and more. It can turn a meal into a feast, a house into a home, a stranger into a friend. It turns problems into gifts, failures into successes, the unexpected into perfect timing, and mistakes into important events. Every person and every situation, big or small, benefits from a dollop of gratitude. As Epictetus said, "He is a wise man who doesn't grieve for the things which he has not, but rejoices for those which he has."

In a society that constantly scrolls and compares, gratitude is more vital than ever. At one point, I stopped practising this ritual, and life quickly began to feel empty. Feelings of inadequacy crept in, filling the spaces where gratitude had once been. It was then that my best friend, Suki, reached out with a gentle suggestion: we would each write down ten things we were grateful for every day and share them.

At first, our lists were filled with the big things: family, health, love. But as we continued, we began to notice the smallest of details – sunlight streaming through a window, the first sip of coffee, a giggle with a friend. Soon, we found ourselves sharing this practice with others, creating a chain of connection. What began as a simple exercise became a movement of love. We eventually turned the practice into a mobile app called With Gratitude, which now helps thousands of people stay committed to this daily ritual of counting blessings.

When we pause each day to give thanks, we begin to tune our energy towards appreciation, and energy always responds in kind. Gratitude works with the lore of resonance and the brain filter system: the more we feel appreciative, the more life reveals new reasons to be so. Regularly thanking the people in our lives softens how we see them; we become kinder, and through the lore of cause and effect, that kindness circles back to us.

By choosing gratitude as the final ritual of the day, we prime ourselves to wake more hopeful, intuitive and attuned. Whatever you dwell on before bed becomes the raw material your brain works with while you sleep. During the night, your mind replays and rewires the emotional tone of the day, which is why bedtime thoughts matter so much. As if we needed more reasons to practise gratitude, research suggests it even heightens intuition, training the mind to notice details and patterns that would otherwise pass unseen.

Magic multiplies in a grateful mind. For any magical practitioner, gratitude isn't optional – it's essential. It forms the foundation of emotional steadiness and energetic alignment, both of which are vital for powerful magic. The Kabbalists teach that whether you've just landed your dream job or been unfairly fired, the one who can return to gratitude, like a steady metronome, will attract the greatest blessings. This is what Dion Fortune meant when she described magic as "the art of changing consciousness at will" – gratitude is the key that makes that possible.

Rituals vs spells

The word spell tends to stir up strong associations. Maybe it conjures bubbling cauldrons, frog tails or wand-waving "hags". Or maybe your mind leaps straight to *Wingardium Leviosa*. But real spells are far more grounded. *Abracadabra*, often dismissed as a magician's catchphrase, actually comes from the ancient Aramaic phrase meaning "I create as I speak." It's not just folklore; it's a profound truth. Words are energetic instruments. Language shapes behaviour and the very reality we experience. In that sense, we're all casting spells through the conversations we have and the ways we speak to ourselves. Just a handful of words can inflame, uplift, deflate or inspire.

Spells are more powerful than thought alone. Unlike fleeting ideas, they require the blend of word, emotion, intention and action. Rituals anchor us in wellbeing. Spells, by contrast, are used more selectively – to call something in, mark a moment, ask for help or create transformation. If you've ever made a wish while blowing out birthday candles, a spell has already been cast. In that moment, your emotion is heightened, it's your birthday and people have just sung to

"All acts of love and pleasure
are my rituals."

– Doreen Valiente

you, and you hold a clear intention, followed by an action to release it into the world. This tradition traces back to ancient Greece: round cakes honoured the Moon, candles symbolised its glow, and smoke was believed to carry wishes skywards to the gods.

In many ways spells echo prayers. Both invite us to reach beyond ourselves and commune with the divine. Where a prayer might be directed towards God, a spell might be woven into the universe, but if God is the Creator, the source of all life, then God and energy begin to sound much the same. Seen this way, a whispered prayer and a whispered spell are kindred acts, two languages calling on the same current of power to be a partner and co-steward in helping us to manifest.

Spells create a concentrated "thought form", an energetic blueprint that, like a stone dropped into still water, ripples outwards. Or think of planting a seed in fertile soil: your spell is the seed, your intention is the water, and your action is the Sun. Evil spells may still haunt fairytales, but in practice, they make no sense to work with. The universal lore of cause and effect cautions why: cause harm, and it will return to you with multiplied force. Magic itself is neutral, it is how we choose to use it that makes all the difference. Every magical worker I've ever met shared this sentiment. Curse someone, and you can expect a curse three times stronger in return. Kabbalistic wisdom goes further still: to slander someone behind their back is not only to generate harmful energy that returns to you, but also to forfeit your own blessings. They believe that the attempt to steal another's light simply transfers to them what was meant for you. The teaching is clear: if you wish to create good fortune for yourself, create good fortune for others by choosing your words, intentions and actions with care.

How to make a spell

Scott Cunningham, pioneering author of over 50 books on Wicca, witchcraft and magic, teaches that a spell is far from supernatural or about demanding things to happen, but a natural process of working with energy to influence outcomes. He writes, "Magic isn't the empty parroting of words and actions; it is an involved, emotionally charged experience in which the words and actions are used as focal points or keys to unlock the power that we all possess."[102]

Here are eight essential ingredients that bring spell work to life:

1. Will

Every effective spell begins with genuine will, a soul-deep desire rooted in purpose. This isn't about whims or surface-level wants. A spell is not a nice-to-have wish list item scribbled in a hurry; it's a message to the universe that says with conviction: "This matters to me deeply, and I won't give up."

Psychosynthesis founder Roberto Assagioli described will not as selfish effort or stubborn push, but as a passionate drive strong enough to direct energy with intention. Will is notably stronger when desire is aligned with something larger than the self. Think of an artist who keeps painting despite rejection, or a mother who studies late into the night to build a better future for her child. Their determination isn't born from greed, but from a calling that benefits others, too. This sort of will gathers scattered impulses, focuses them, and points them toward what truly matters.

Everyone I spoke to warned against using spells purely to fuel consumerist greed, because of the unexpected consequences that often arise. "New practitioners arrive at spellwork seeing it as a hack to acquire things – more money, a relationship, fancy cars or greater beauty – but this approach inherently stems from a sense of lack or scarcity", Druidcraft founder Philip Carr-Gomm shared with me. Falling into greed from a place of lack just ends up attracting more lack, though it may appear in disguise. For example, let's say you perform a spell to get more money, but the sudden wealth strains your relationships. The person seeking money might gain funds but at the cost of community and peace of mind. You've simply swapped one feeling of lack for another.

Spells cast with strong will connected to a greater cause carry momentum. I once asked a successful entrepreneur, who had studied Kabbalah for over 20 years, whether he was frustrated that another company's rapid success had overtaken his own. He replied: "No. That guy had more determination for success than I did." The next time someone else seems to move ahead, ask yourself how strong your will truly is, and what's driving it. The strength and quality of your determination, and the why behind it, are directly tied to the results you'll get. As the old saying goes: where there is a will, there is a way.

2. Emotional frequency

The emotion behind a spell is what charges it. The stronger your emotional charge, the more potent the spell.

If your emotional field is tangled in guilt, jealousy or resentment, despite strong will, the spell may backfire or simply fizzle. A spell for abundance cast while secretly feeling like a failure, through resonance, might only deepen the feeling of failure. When a spell is cast from joy, creativity or service, it carries that frequency and the universe reads that signal and responds in kind. Energy doesn't judge; it mirrors. Choose the emotional frequency very carefully, and one that aligns with what you want to pull in.

Raising your vibration before spellwork is critical for success. Try gratitude journaling, dancing, yoga, breathwork, or a walk in nature to immerse yourself in natural beauty. Music, too, is a potent frequency shifter, it entrains your heartbeat, breath, and mood, aligning your energy to the rhythm of your intention. These small rituals help bring your inner state into harmony with what you're calling in.

Witch and author Rebecca Beattie recommends entering a flow state before any spellwork. She suggests turning your favourite activity into a spell from painting, cooking, singing, writing, or moving. "Spell cookies" is one of my favourites (more on which shortly). When you do something you love, joy and gratitude naturally rise, and your intention becomes infused with that higher vibration. I've even used my spinning class as a perfect spell container.

The foundational rule for magic and spell-work is simple: the energy you put into a spell determines the energy that comes out of your spell. So, it is essential to intentionally create or raise your energy before you start.

3. Having a vivid mental picture

Good spells need clear directions, and that's where visualisation comes in – a practice shared by athletes, healers, high performers, and yes, witches. It trains both the mind and body to recognise opportunity when it appears. Jim Carrey famously wrote himself a $10 million cheque for "acting services rendered" long before he got his break, carrying it in his wallet until it came true.

Why does this work? Because the brain doesn't know the difference between a real event and a vividly imagined one. A scary film can raise your heartbeat. So can an imagined future. As Lynne McTaggart, the intention expert, said to me during our interview, "Your brain is so smart in so many ways, but it's also a little bit dumb, it can't tell the difference between action and thought." When you imagine running, the same neurons fire as if you were actually doing it. That's why elite athletes use visualisation; it's training without movement.

Visualisation doesn't just change how you feel, it communicates to every cell in your body and influences how your body responds. In one clinical trial, patients who used guided imagery before surgery reported less pain and lower anxiety, and required fewer painkillers.[103]

In today's world of constant interruption, we shortchange ourselves by not creating enough time to dream and imagine. Imagination is like a muscle, the more you use it, the stronger it becomes. Before engaging in spell work, give your mind space to wander and strengthen vivid mental pictures.

One of the most powerful moments to practice visualisation is just before sleep. As mentioned already, whatever you focus on before drifting off is what your brain continues to process during the night. The reverse is also true: if you fall asleep replaying anger or frustration, the neural pathways connected to those feelings strengthen, making it easier to feel triggered the next day.

Protect pre-sleep time and practise letting your mind cast itself into a land of imagination, where every dream of your future feels possible.

4. Focus

Your spell needs focus – sustained and clear attention. A big obstacle to successful spellcasting is scattered thinking. We send out a wish, then immediately cloud it with doubt, distraction or multiple competing desires. This fragmented energy weakens the spell. Focus is power.

Most spells don't manifest because we have conflicting intentions. For example, someone might wish for a bigger house but also crave more work–life balance, two desires that could pull in different directions. Or someone might want an intimate relationship but also want autonomy. If you're divided, so is the energy behind your spell.

Abraham Hicks teaches that holding a thought for just 17 seconds helps activate focus and thus its momentum. It might sound brief, but in a world of pings and pop-ups, even 17 seconds of focused thought is rare. Neuroscience supports this: when we concentrate on a thought infused with emotion, we begin to influence our own brain filters. Even a few moments of undivided attention can help prime your biology, retrain your Reticular Activating System (RAS), and reshape what you notice, feel, and resonate with.

If a single sad thought can make you cry or feel anxious, that's proof of your internal power. When your energy, mind and body align around a single clear direction, your external reality will shift.

5. Knowledge

Magic is not guesswork nor the stuff of only fairytales. Behind every successful spell is a framework of understanding – of timing, symbols, natural rhythms and spiritual principles. Knowledge might include which herbs to use, which candle colour aligns with the intention, or how moon phases and specific planetary alignments influence energy. You don't need to know everything, but you do need to know what you're doing and why. Just like cooking, you can follow a basic recipe, but understanding the ingredients transforms the outcome. You will find examples below.

6. Action

Spells are not passive. They set energy in motion, but you are part of that motion. The universe is your partner, not your genie. You cast the spell, and then you step towards it. As Lynne McTaggart reminded me, "You can visualise healing but you still need to book the doctor's appointment."

Visualisation plants the seed. Action waters it. Imagine spellwork as a curling stone, you set it in motion, but your actions are the broom that buffers it towards your desired destination.

7. Playfulness and humility

These are often the most overlooked ingredients in spell-casting. However, there is no doubt that spells work better when you enjoy them. The brain learns faster through play. The renowned child development expert Dr Karyn Purvis once said, "It takes approximately 400 repetitions to create a new synapse in the brain, unless it's done in play, in which case it takes just 10 to 20."[104] Magic doesn't respond to force. It responds to joy, movement, humour – these uplift your vibration and reduce resistance.

A witch once told me she writes "magic potions" on her perfume bottles. When she sprays them in the morning, she says it feels like casting a spell. That's the essence of magical thinking: small, fun, sincere gestures that ripple with meaning.

As a child, I remember wishing every single night for a horse. I waited for years – then, one day, my parents were asked to look after a friend's very old donkey in their back garden. The wish came true ... sort of. Magic has a sense of humour. Be open to the giggle.

It's important to remember that we do not own our blessings; they are only ever on temporary loan. With this awareness, every gift becomes sacred, and every answered spell an invitation to care for, honour, and share what has been entrusted to us. Magic, above all, requires humility. The moment we grow complacent is the moment we lose our power.

"Magic is a prayer with
will behind it."

– Dion Fortune

8. Living like a spell

Spells, like prayers, don't always get answered in the way we imagine. The path to our wished-for outcome may take us through unexpected steps, so we must remain open to whatever arrives, knowing a spell is still unfolding. Just as you can't bake a cake without first breaking an egg, sometimes a spell's success requires challenges to appear alongside blessings.

If you cast a spell for greater peace and love in your life, for example, this might cause toxic relationships to dissolve. That process could be uncomfortable and stressful. Or if you create a spell for a dream job, you might receive it … along with long hours and new demands. Change rarely comes without its own side effects, the saying "be careful what you wish for" couldn't be more accurate.

Don't give up on your spell too quickly, either. When challenges arrive, know you are in the middle of making something beautiful. Just like baking, magic requires a little bit of mess – and, most of all, patience. Spells might not always look like sparkles and rainbows, but with magical perseverance, they will create them in the end. At its core, magic is guided by ethics as much as intention. Occult author Susan Bowes reminds us of this, writing, "As long as you adhere to the sacred law of magic making, which is never to manipulate another person against their will, you cannot go wrong."

Final spell reminders

Remember, all magic and spells work *in harmony* with natural laws. If you're expecting magical results for something that nature can't do, you're unlikely to have good results. For example, if I wanted to be an NBA basketball player, no amount of magic can make this happen. Nature did not bless me as a 6-foot-7 shooter who's 22 years old. Work *with* nature rather than battling against it.

Magic isn't reserved for ancient scrolls or mythical spells. It's here, humming beneath the surface of your ordinary days, waiting to be activated through meaning, intention and joy. When you build rituals, cast spells or simply whisper a wish into your coffee steam, you're choosing to be intentional and to participate in shaping your reality. Spells are acts of self-empowerment. Instead of waiting to be rescued, you're consciously activating your power as a co-creator. With clarity, curiosity and a touch of playfulness, you hold the ability to create good fortune.

Moon power

Timing matters in spell work. For thousands of years, the Moon has been a guide for rituals, symbolising different energies throughout its cycle. Each phase carries a unique signature that influences the outcome of your spell work.

- **New moon:** A blank slate. The best time to plant seeds, set intentions, dream big and get quiet enough to hear your soul speak.
- **Waxing moon:** Growth and momentum. Use this time to draw things in – money, love, courage, clarity, healing.
- **Full moon:** A peak moment of power. Emotions rise, truth surfaces and energy amplifies. It's ideal for release, gratitude, forgiveness, and reflection.
- **Waning moon:** Let go. This is the time to banish bad habits, toxic energy and anything no longer serving your highest good.

Indigenous and Eastern traditions recognise the Moon's pull on sea tides as a mirror for its impact on human energy. Spell work that aligns with these rhythms works like a sail catching the wind, it gives you a nice easy breeze to move in the direction you want.

For a deeper practice, I recommend Dr Kate Tomas's lunar calendar. Her guidance on timing can add subtle yet significant power to your rituals.

Tools and props

Candles, crystals, herbs and oils are beautiful amplifiers of intention, but remember, they're just tools. The magic comes from you.

Candles are one of the simplest and most powerful. They symbolise illumination, transformation and the divine spark within. Choose your colour wisely:

- White for peace and clarity
- Pink for love and friendship
- Red for courage or sensuality
- Green for abundance and fertility
- Blue for healing and truth
- Yellow for creativity
- Purple for intuition
- Orange for opportunity
- Silver for psychic work

Always let your ritual candle burn down completely. Don't reuse decorative candles or night-lights for spells as they hold a different energetic signature. Use matches if you can; wood connects with earth's energy.

Oils are another ancient and sacred tool. They've been used in sacred ceremonies for millennia. Rosemary, lavender, frankincense, jasmine, and myrrh each carry a specific vibration. While essential oils work beautifully, handmade blends you create yourself carry even more power. The act of crafting something with intention infuses it with magic from the very first step.

Glamour magic: attraction spells

Beauty and spell craft are ideal magical companions – a way of weaving intention, energy, and presence into what you wear, how you move, and how you use creams and perfumes each day.

The very word *glamour* comes from Celtic magic, where it described an enchantment that altered perception, casting a shimmer over reality so that others saw what the witch wished them to see. What began as a spell of illusion later slipped into language as "style" or "allure," but at its heart, glamour has always meant enchantment.

Dr Kate Tomas says that "anything containing a molecule of water can be enchanted". To try this, rub your hands together until you feel heat rising in your palms. That warmth is energy. Hold your hands over your beauty products, perhaps your favourite moisturiser, and speak an intention: "Help this cream make me radiant in my most authentic self." Each time you use the product, you're not just tending to your skin, you're charging your energy field.

Perfume should always be a potion. Before you spray, rub your hands, infuse the bottle with energy and whisper your desire. With every spritz, your spell travels through scent, magnifying presence and drawing attention to you in subtle, magnetic ways.

"Lipstick is really magical. It holds
more than a waxy bit of colour –
it holds the promise of a brilliant smile,
and a brilliant day, both literally
and figuratively."

– *Charlotte Tilbury*

Whispers for perfume spells

- "Spritz me with protection; let me repel all negativity and the evil eye."
- "Spritz me with magnetism; may aligned opportunities flow easily towards me."
- "Spritz me with courage; may my voice be strong and my presence felt."
- "Spritz me with clarity; let me see truth and act with wisdom."
- "Spritz me with joy; may my energy uplift all who cross my path."
- "Spritz me with abundance; may I walk through open doors and fertile ground."
- "Spritz me with calm; let serenity surround me in every encounter."
- "Spritz me with allure; may my presence draw kindness, respect and love."

Clothes can also carry enchantment. A coat can become armour, a dress an invocation, a favourite piece of jewellery a talisman. As Dr Tomas teaches, glamour magic is the art of making the ordinary extraordinary by imbuing it with intention. These types of spell are ancient arts. It is not about hiding who you are or manipulating with negative intent; it's simply about amplifying your essence.

Morning tea spell

A daily brew to energise your intention and set the tone for your day.

Prepare your morning tea or coffee with a moment of mindfulness. As the water boils, whisper an intention into it – something simple and true, like:

> May I be at peace today. May my energy be settled.

As you stir in honey, milk, or lemon, speak your wish again with a smile:

> This cup holds peace and calm for me,
> A spell of love in sip and tea.

Drink slowly, letting the warmth remind you that you're starting the day with presence and power.

Spell cookies

Intention

These cookies aren't just nourishing snacks, they're edible spells. Each ingredient holds symbolic meaning, and the act of mixing, stirring, baking and blessing them becomes a magical ritual to align your energy with your desires. Whether you need more love, grounding, confidence or clarity, make these cookies to feed both your body and spirit.

You'll need:
(You can adapt based on your mood, intention or pantry.)
- 1 cup (90g) oats – **grounding and stabilising**
- 1 mashed banana – **sweetness and joy**
- 2 tbsp nut butter – **inner strength and self-worth**
- 1 tbsp honey or maple syrup – **sweetness and love**
- A pinch of ground cinnamon – **passion and vitality**

- A handful of dark chocolate chips or berries – **magic and delight**

Method

1. **Set your intention.**
   Before you begin, pause. What do you want these cookies to bring into your life? Peace? Confidence? Love? Speak it aloud or write it on a small piece of paper to keep near you as you bake.

2. **Bless your ingredients.**
   As you lay out each ingredient, say a small blessing. For example:

   Oats for grounding, may I stand strong.
   Banana for joy, may lightness fill my heart.
   Nut butter for strength, may I feel secure in myself.
   Cinnamon for passion, may I burn bright with purpose.
   Chocolate for delight, may I never forget the magic in life.

3. **Stir with intention.**
   As you combine the ingredients in a bowl, stir clockwise (to draw something in), repeating your intention aloud or in your mind. For example:

   May each bite bring [peace/love/success]. I stir this spell into being.

4. **Shape the cookies.**
   As you form the dough into cookies, press your intention into each one. You might whisper a wish or affirmation through the dough:

I am safe.
Love flows to me easily.
I shine with creative confidence.

5   **Bake and bless.**
Bake at 180°C / 350°F for 10–12 minutes, or until golden. As they bake, visualise the oven alchemising your ingredients and intentions into something sacred.

6.   **Eat with presence.**
When the cookies are cool, eat one slowly. Let it be a sensory experience – a ritual of receiving. Offer one to someone else you love, if you feel called. Share the magic.

The World is the tarot's grand finale. It speaks of completion, mastery and the deep satisfaction of reaching a long-awaited milestone. The World whispers, "You've come full circle" and embodies unity between self, others and the universe. Beyond this moment of arrival lies the invitation to begin again, carrying the wisdom you have earned.

Epilogue
The good fortune game

"He had no obvious reason to celebrate his life. And yet
he did, and knowing he had no reason to celebrate his life
made him exult all the more. How joyous this life is! How
grateful he was to be alive, and to share that joy and fun
and delight with others."

– Adam Robinson

My entry into the world of magic felt like tumbling down
Alice's rabbit hole or stepping on to Dorothy's yellow brick
road. Subtle signs winked at me to follow, invisible forces
revealed themselves, and suddenly, the world appeared
different. Cups of coffee were no longer just coffee; they
became purposeful morning rituals that set the tone for
my day. Exercise classes became energy-raising ceremonies,
supercharging my spells. The Moon wasn't just a distant
celestial body, it was a cosmic clock, tracking the rhythm
of my days. Coincidences no longer existed, only meaningful synchronicities signposting the way forward. Morning
commutes became sacred opportunities to salute the trees
lining my route and nod to the daffodils that welcomed
spring. Living a magical life transforms not only how you
see the world, but how the world responds to you. There is
no such thing as an ending when you're magical. You start to

realise that what seems an ending is just a transition into a new realm, an adjusted timeline, or a metamorphosis into a better version of yourself.

At first, it's bewildering to learn that trees communicate, flowers hold energy, and that an internal shift can rewire your entire reality. But as the magic unfolds, life feels both exciting and reassuring. A deep, wise intuition awakens within, the knowing that all will be well and every challenge is perfectly designed for our elevation. As Carl Jung wrote, "In all chaos there is a cosmos, in all disorder a secret order."

Learning to rewrite the rules

Becoming magical is a choice; one that requires you to honour the lores of the unseen world. When you do, good fortune follows. I first learned this from a brilliant witch I met in New York. On the surface, he has advised some of the world's most influential financiers, but beneath this, he has lived a life of magic. Our first meeting lasted three hours, during which he was both ethereal and matter-of-fact, offering a rare combination of grounded wisdom and otherworldly insight. Somewhere between coffee and dessert, he leaned forward and said, "I think you are ready to start playing The Magical Game." My fascination was palpable. The great witch proceeded to share his tried-and-tested formula for working in harmony with cosmic forces to activate magic daily. Over the course of half a century, this formula has enabled him to live the most exciting, abundant, enchanted life, and now I have the privilege of passing on his wisdom.

Principle one: Connect with "The Other"

"The Other?" I asked, puzzled. "Who's that?" He smiled. "The Other is anyone and everyone you meet. It takes two people – you and The Other – to create a cosmic circuit, unleashing unimaginable powers." At first, this principle contradicted much of the new-age spirituality I had encountered. So much of the self-help world focuses on inner work, personal boundaries, and self-development in isolation. But this witch advocated that true growth comes not from self-focus but from shifting attention to others. "By connecting with others, you prevent yourself from sleepwalking through life, not noticing what's going on around you. Focusing on others pulls you out of your own self-indulgent mind – the place where anxiety, doubt and over-analysis breed. It is only with your eyes open that you can activate the universe's energy."

He leaned back and explained, "People often tell me, 'You're so confident.' But I'm not confident. Then again, I'm not afraid either. I'm just completely focused on the person in front of me or the task at hand. If your attention is fully on another person, you don't have time to worry about how you look, how you sound or whether you belong."

This struck a deep chord. Most of my anxiety came from worrying about how I was being perceived, robbing me of the ability to keep my eyes open and be fully present. But when I applied this principle, I noticed something change. "Whenever you feel anxious, bored or irritated", the witch said, "that's your cue to shift your focus – either to a task or to another person. At a social event, you can either spiral into self-consciousness about your outfit, which is an immediate off-switch for magic, or you can ask a question and lose yourself in someone else's story. When you get out of your head and into the moment, fear and anxiety don't have room to stretch their claws."

This principle also reveals why magic is often easier to tap in to in unfamiliar places. Have you ever noticed how you have better ideas and feel more creatively alive when on holiday or in a place you don't know well? There's a reason for this. When we travel, we are forced to place our attention on "The Other" – other things, other people, other places. We have to consult a map to find the places we want to go, forcing us away from mindless autopilot mode. We notice new buildings, smell unfamiliar scents, and observe the smallest of details with fresh eyes. But in familiar settings, the streets you've walked a hundred times blur into the background, and instead of looking out, you assume you've seen it before and go back to scrolling. How can the universe wink at you when you're looking at your phone or lost in the spiral of worries?

You don't need to be on holiday to experience synchronicities or spot opportunities. You just need to use that holiday mentality of keeping your eyes open and focusing on "The Other" in your day-to-day life, opening the cosmic circuit for potential.

"On this journey, it's important to realise that everyone you meet is a potential key, never an accident", the witch said. At first glance, connecting with others seems simple. But in practice, judgement, prejudice and preconceptions can make it a significant challenge. True magic lies in releasing judgement. Not just of others, but of ourselves, too, because we don't really know where we've been or where we're going. Rather than becoming frustrated with difficult colleagues, family members, partners, politicians or even strangers, we can view every interaction as a mirror reflecting an insight. Instead of asking, "Why is this person so irritating?" shift the question to: "Why is this person in my life? What are they here to teach me?" We learn more about ourselves from our adversaries than from our allies. Yet, the unconscious mind tends to attack the mirror, without realising that it may be a perfectly placed key to unlock the next level.

The witch explained: "If you want to change how the world behaves towards you, start by changing how you understand your interactions with it."

Admittedly, not passing judgement is much easier said than done. If you can't immediately find the learning in a difficult interaction, perhaps the simplest approach is to "let them", as Mel Robbins puts it. Letting go of the need to control, correct or change someone is its own act of magic.

The witch's first magical principle reminded me of a book I read as a teenager: Mitch Albom's *The Five People You Meet in Heaven*. The book tells the story of the afterlife, where, upon dying, you meet five people who have shaped your life in profound ways, even if you never realised it at the time. Often, we assume only big, dramatic relationships shape our destiny. But the smallest, most fleeting encounters can change the course of our lives without us realising. What if the stranger you dismissed was actually the one who nudged you unknowingly towards a critical decision? What if a brief exchange saved you from a path you were about to fatally walk down?

It makes you wonder about all the lives you've unknowingly touched, and all those who've quietly shaped yours without realising. This was the heart of the witch's first lesson: if the universe works through people, then every connection is a potential portal of information. I was reminded of the late spiritual teacher Karen Berg, who passionately listened and asked for everyone's opinion, from the intern to a CEO. She recognised that each person could act as a channel for insight. If the universe wants to speak, it often does so through other people.

Principle two: Seek to create fun and delight for "The Other"

After the third cup of tea, the mystical witch embarked on sharing his second principle for activating magic. "We cannot expect miracles by demanding them," he continued. "Instead, we have to make it our mission to bring the people we meet joy and share as abundantly as possible." At first, this sounded overly altruistic and draining, but the witch quickly clarified: "I'm not talking about selflessness. This is where people go wrong. When you look to create miracles for others, you create more for yourself. For example, imagine you are in a job interview. What's your goal?" the witch asked.

"To get the job," I replied with some confusion.

"Nope," he smiled. "Your only goal is to connect with the person in front of you and make the experience enjoyable for them. If you do that, they'll remember you – whether it's for the role you applied for, or something else later down the line. Every interaction, whether with a stranger on a train, a friend, a family member or a waiter at a café, offers an opportunity to activate the law of resonance. Every interaction is a mirror, a chance to magnetise what you most desire. Magical people don't just connect with The Other; they leave The Other feeling better than when they arrived," he whispered.

He was right, thoughtfulness costs nothing – yet it creates a powerful, energetic domino effect of positive impact. Holding a door open, buying the person behind you a coffee, making a cup of tea for someone at work, organising a really fun date or simply remembering someone's birthday can transform someone's day – and yours. Compliments are energetic gifts you can never run out of. "Principle two is such a fun principle to live by," the witch said. "By making the effort to make a stranger or friend feel special, you make yourself irresistibly attractive to the universe, which cannot help but send you back good fortune after good fortune. And while creating fun and delight for others, don't forget to create it for yourself."

"But what if you constantly help people, and they don't help you back?" I asked. His answer was profound. "You keep going. Other people aren't your business partners – the universe is. Every positive act you share accumulates, and the universe will return it. No one is shortchanged. It's the law of cause and effect. It may not be immediate or even happen in this lifetime, and it may not return in the way you expect, but it will always return." Give fearlessly and without regret, knowing the universe is keeping score. That is true magic. After a difficult month, I'll often have a quiet word and say, "OK universe, you've sent me a lot of challenges, I am now ready for the blessings." It never ceases to amaze me how many times something wonderful will then happen, however small.

The witch described this as "level two" spirituality, moving beyond simply asking for what we want to *giving what we want*. When we focus on helping others to create their dreams in any way we can, the universe aligns in service to us, and our own hopes and wishes start unfolding at an accelerated rate. This is how you become a channel for love, and often how other people receive the very answers they have prayed for. Our dreams become the seeds of someone else's, and theirs become the seeds of ours.

When I asked to meet this masterful witch, little did I know I was engaging in principle one. By meeting me for dessert, the witch fulfilled principle two – cake is far more delightful and fun than a quick phone call. He gave up his time to teach a randomer the secrets behind his magic. It was a life-altering meeting and the start of a valuable friendship.

"We cannot get without giving.
In working magic, we expend our own
pyschological and emotional
energy and must take care to replenish
it. Magic is an art and a discipline
that demands work, practice and effort
before it can be perfected."

– *Starhawk*

We often associate giving with monetary gifts, but offering time, love, thoughtfulness, skills or acts of kindness is often far more valuable. True abundance begins when you make it your mission to be a weaver of miracles for others, creating a ripple effect that returns to you multiplied, filling your life with wonder. The universe thrives on reciprocity. The more you offer to the world, the more it flows back to you. As the ancient Kabbalists write, "The only way to receive the Light is to become like the Light – to share."

A good example of this is when brands offer a free gift with a purchase. The idea of receiving something extra for free encourages someone to buy. Estée Lauder was the first entrepreneur to implement such a strategy in the 1950s. At first, her husband questioned the logic. Estée understood that giving is never in vain; it's the engine of creation. Her generosity became the secret key to building one of the world's first multibillion-dollar beauty empires. But her success was more than strategy – it was spiritual. In response to her husband's worry about giving too much away, she writes about how she'd reassure him: "Don't you worry … whatever we give away, God will give back to us."[105] And that is exactly what happened.

Principle three: Expect magic everywhere

Principle three builds on what this book has already explored in depth: the law of assumption. Our assumptions shape the filters of the brain and, in turn, the reality we experience. When we expect magic to unfold, not only in spells or rituals, but in the ordinary moments of daily life, we unlock the most essential ingredient for turning life itself into a magical game.

The witch explained it like this: "Now, we all live by a set of rules. And life unfolds according to the rules you hold, consciously or not." He let the words settle before asking, "How would you describe work, Poppy?" I thought for a moment before answering: "A bit stressful, sometimes unfair, but brain-stimulating … and a doorway to freedom." He nodded. "OK, well that's exactly how work will continue to show up for you. Our minds are designed to seek evidence that confirms what we *already* believe. But here's the magic – you can rewrite those beliefs and find new evidence. Your current rules for life were likely built from real experiences, but just because something has been true before, doesn't mean it must be true forever. If you're not content with how life is unfolding, change the evidence your brain looks for, change your assumptions. The moment you assume 'I am magical, a master of energy, capable of shaping my reality' is the moment your brain looks for evidence to confirm it. Life mirrors your beliefs back at you."

To be living a life of good fortune constantly is to believe, deeply and consistently, that the universe is always conspiring in your favour. Even when you face a challenge – rejection, financial pressure, heartbreak, health scares, or worry for loved ones – there is, of course, tremendous pain. But if you can believe with certainty that these difficult realities are all an opportunity to become better – wiser, stronger, softer and more resilient, your brain filters will change, and miracles will be revealed. Whenever I've called a wise witch to share my bad news or a painful experience, their first response has always been: "I am so happy for you, a huge blessing *must* be waiting." At first, the positivity in the face of hardship feels strange, even jarring. But over time, I've come to see that every difficulty carries within it the seed of something good.

Magic isn't passive or a waiting game for luck to strike your path. It's a discipline that turns life into a proactive practice of creating good fortune. You can take what happens to you, wallow in the pain, and let it turn into destructive patterns. Or you can choose time and again to feel the pain and transmute it into a story that elevates you and benefits others. Like yoga, participation builds magical muscles – and with them, the inner power to shape reality. This is what Dion Fortune captured so simply all those years ago: magic is the art of changing consciousness at will.

A magical life

Magic is everywhere. The feeling of singing alongside sixty thousand people at Wembley. The heart tingle when a stranger does something kind. The delirious joy of dissolving into laughter with a friend long after you have forgotten the joke. The quiet comfort of sitting beside someone you love and no words are required. The peace of walking through the woods, hearing the whistle of the breeze. The wonder of a sunset. The felt sense of a past loved one looking over you.

These are life's magical moments. And yet, they slip from view when competition, status and hierarchy take hold. We do not need more "successful" people, sad souls in expensive restaurants or crowded rooms. We need more intuitive beings, who notice and create magic for themselves and others. People who dance to their own rhythm, listen to the earth, those who revel in the small beauties of life, knowing they are the big beauties. We need more *witches*.

The next time the world feels like it is ending, pause to remember. Somewhere, somehow, some magical, intuitive human is already dreaming about an idea that could transform everything.

When you open yourself to the unseen world of energy,

magic happens. When you release rigid timelines and follow the synchronicities guiding you, magic happens. When you lean into your desires, recognising them as sacred callings, magic happens. When you connect and create delight for others, magic happens. When you give unconditionally and remember the universe is your business partner, magic happens. When you strengthen your intuition and find meaning in dreams, magic happens. When you consciously live in harmony with the cycles of nature, magic happens. When you expand your understanding of what's possible, magic happens.

So, what's the real secret? Everyone carries a witch within, an innate capacity to create and experience magic.

——————— * ———————

And now, you're at 0, a fresh start, the beginning
of endless possibilities.

Let go of the conditioning that makes you afraid,
nervous or cynical. Stay open. Magic happens when
reality defies logic. Remember: 95 per cent of reality is
still waiting to be discovered.

Move forwards with a knowing.

A knowing that magic is waiting to be activated.

Trust in the journey back to yourself. This is where
your inner power and true fortune lies.

Welcome to your magical life.

——————— * ———————

Acknowledgements

I am writing this under a full moon, which feels fitting, since full moons are cosmic invitations to pause and give thanks.

Firstly, I owe the creation of this book to Rebecca Nicolson, and to Jessie Inchauspé for introducing us. Rebecca emailed me a couple of times asking if I was ready to write a book, and when I finally knew I wanted to write a love poem to the witches who had changed my life and share their wisdom, she immediately supported the vision. A book celebrating and redefining what it means to be magical could have easily been met with hesitation, but Rebecca, and Aurea Carpenter, at New River Books welcomed me in with open hearts. From our very first meeting, I knew I was sitting with two powerful witches.

This process has felt unlike any project I have ever worked on. Having lived across three cities and built companies in technology, health and fashion, this book has represented something deeper – a soul calling. I have had the immense privilege of working with Helena Sutcliffe, whose patience, encouragement, and willingness to read draft after draft have been beyond generous.

There has not been a single day I have not loved writing this book. Each time I sat down to immerse myself in the ancient wisdom of the witches, I felt inspired, guided and protected by their energy. I hope you feel that too as you read these pages. There are many witches by my definition – magical, intuitive, cosmic people – who deserve a special mention. Deike Begg is the first. She is the author of

Synchronicity, one of my favourite books in the world, and she has given me countless hours of her time and insight. Deike has read my tarot for nearly eight years, and just sitting in her presence, learning about Jung, psychosynthesis and the cards' sacred symbolism has been life-changing. I would arrive at her home and leave many hours later feeling completely renewed and lit up by the possibilities of life. Her breadth of knowledge, spanning science, psychology, mythology and magic, continues to inspire me.

The second witch is Ruth Nahmias, a Kabbalistic astrologer and spiritual teacher who has guided me for more than 15 years. When I am in crisis, her ability to hold both pain and faith, trusting that blessings are always hidden within difficulty, feels like pure soul medicine. The spiritual training I have received through her has shaped everything. Without Ruth, my life would look very different. I would likely be chasing the wrong things and having emotional meltdowns as regularly as the British rain. If you're interested in learning more, I recommend exploring the online courses at www.kabbalah.com or attending in-person classes at one of their centres around the world.

The third witch is my mother, the most magical woman I know. She can turn a situation around faster than Sabrina the Teenage Witch could click her fingers and get dressed. Her enthusiasm for life is contagious. The word "enthusiasm" is interesting as it has divine roots from the Greek word *enthousiasmos*, meaning "to be inspired or possessed by a god". My mother is the living embodiment of that word. Her delight in the smallest details, like spotting a robin outside her window, can brighten even the bleakest day. My father, after 40 years by her side, is well on his way to becoming a witch himself, though I doubt I will see him swinging a pendulum anytime soon. And speaking of pendulums, I must thank my mother's. Its uncanny accuracy has offered comfort and clarity when my intuition has fallen quiet.

To all the witches featured in this book: Dr Christina Oakley Harrington, founder of Treadwells, whose magical bookshop in London should be a pilgrimage site for anyone drawn to magical teachings. Its walls hum with energy. Dr Vivianne Crawley, whose writings and workshops are portals to new dimensions of understanding. Dion Fortune, a pioneer of her time, who spoke courageously about mystical truth when it was dangerous for women to do so. And Dr Kate Tomas, whose workshops, especially on magical seduction, are transformative.

A heartfelt recognition also to Rupert Sheldrake, whose groundbreaking research into consciousness and intuition continues to challenge scientific orthodoxy. Despite criticism, his courage to explore the unseen has given legitimacy to ideas that once lived only in the margins.

A big thank you to Esther Palmer, who created the most beautiful illustrations for this book. She made my words come to life with her exquisite art and I couldn't be happier.

I also want to thank Alia Coster, who helped me bring order to my tangled thoughts and helped me clarify ephemeral ideas.

And, of course, my partner Jack Bryant. Thank you for your endless patience, for answering the door to yet another delivery of witch books, for living with a kitchen table covered in candles, tarot decks and spell ingredients, and for letting me drag you to the wackiest healers without questioning. You have been the kindest support and a great grounding force.

Finally, thank you to you, for opening these pages and stepping into this world with me. I hope this book inspires you to embrace the mystery of life and to remember that endless possibilities await. With a little passion, energy and expectation of miracles, I hope you now know the world begins to look and feel very different.

References

The words on these pages have been influenced through conversation, research and the wisdom of others. It's essential to acknowledge them, not only to give credit for their impactful insights but also to point out helpful further reading on your magical journey. In recognising these contributions, I hope to share the path I've walked with the guidance of brilliant minds and inspire your own exploration into the realms of magic, self-discovery and transformation.

Dr Jeanne Achterberg: *Imagery in Healing: Shamanism and Modern Medicine* (1985).

Mitch Albom: *The Five People You Meet in Heaven* (2003).

Dolores Ashcroft-Nowicki: *The Magical Use of Thought Forms* (2001).

Roberto Assagioli: *Psychosynthesis: A Manual of Principles and Techniques* (1965).

Roberto Assagioli: *Psychosynthesis: A Collection of Basic Writings* (1975).

Roberto Assagioli: *Transpersonal Development* (2007).

Deike Begg: *Synchronicity: The Art of Coincidence, Choice, and Unlocking Your Mind* (2010).

Monica Berg: *Fear Is Not an Option* (2017).

Susan Bowes: *The Wiccan Handbook* (2003).

Lois Bourne: *Witch Amongst Us: The Autobiography of a Witch* (1979).

Rhonda Byrne: *The Magic* (2012).

Joseph Campbell: *The Hero with a Thousand Faces* (1949).

Philipp Carr-Gomm: *Druidcraft: The Magic of Wicca and Druidry* (2002).

Paulo Coelho: *The Alchemist* (1988).

Dr Vivianne Crowley: *The Magical Life: A Wiccan Priestess Shares Her Secrets* (1994). *Wicca: The Old Religion in the New Millennium* (1989). *Wild Once* (2024).

Phyllis Curott: *Book of Shadows* (1998).

Barbara Ehrenreich and Deirdre English: *Witches, Midwives, and Nurses: A History of Women Healers* (1973).

Silvia Federici: *Caliban and the Witch: Women, the Body and Primitive Accumulation* (2004).

Leon Festinger: *A Theory of Cognitive Dissonance* (1957).

Dion Fortune: *Applied Magic* (2000 edition).

Matilda Gage: *Woman, Church, and State* (1893).

Chris Gosden: *The History of Magic: From Alchemy to Witchcraft, from the Ice Age to the Present* (2020).

Philippa Gregory: *Normal Women: 900 Years of Making History* (2023).

Graham Harvey: *Animism: Respecting the Living World* (2005).

Werner Heisenberg: *The Physical Principles of the Quantum Theory* (1930).

Laura Lynne Jackson: *Signs: The Secret Language of the Universe* (2019).

Carl Jung: *Synchronicity: An Acausal Connecting Principle* (1952).

Elisabeth Kübler-Ross: *On Life After Death* (1991).

Dr William Li: *Eat to Beat Disease: The New Science of How Your Body Can Heal Itself* (2019).

Lisa Miller: *The Awakened Brain: The New Science of Spirituality and Our Quest for an Inspired Life* (2021).

Dr Raymond Moody: *Life After Life: The Investigation of a Phenomenon – Survival of Bodily Death* (1975).

Tom Myers: *Anatomy Trains: Myofascial Meridians for Manual and Movement Therapists* (2001).

Ruth Nahmias: Kabbalistic Astrology with Ruth Nahmias – https://www.youtube.com/@ruth.nahmias

Michael Norton: *The Ritual Effect* (2024).

Yoko Ono: Interview, Pitchfork (2007).

Dr Christina Oakley-Harrington: *Plant Magic* (2020) and *Dreams of Witches* (2023).

Marcel Proust: *In Search of Lost Time* (1913–1927).

J. K. Rowling: *Harry Potter and the Chamber of Secrets* (1998).

Rupert Sheldrake: *A New Science of Life: The Hypothesis of Formative Causation* (1981). *The Presence of the Past: Morphic Resonance and the Habits of Nature* (1988). *The Rebirth of Nature: The Greening of Science and God* (1991). *Science and Spiritual Practices:*

Transformative Experiences and Their Effects on Our Bodies, Brains, and Health (2017).
Rudolf Steiner: *Anthroposophy in Everyday Life* (1912/1995).
Regina Tomasheva: *Pussy: A Reclamation* (2016).
Dr Kate Tomas: Magical Seduction Masterclass – www.drkatetomas. com.
Taylor Swift: *Reputation* album, song "I Did Something Bad" (2017).
Pim van Lommel: *Consciousness Beyond Life: The Science of the Near-Death Experience* (2010).
Bessel van der Kolk: *The Body Keeps the Score: Brain, Mind, and Body in the Healing of Trauma* (2014).
Benebell Wen: *Holistic Tarot: An Integrative Approach to Using Tarot for Personal Growth* (2015).
Professor Richard Wiseman: *The Luck Factor: The Scientific Study of the Lucky Mind* (2004).
Vivienne Wild: *Wild Once* (2024).
Josh Williams: *Spiritual Herbalism: The Magic and Medicine of the Plants* (2021).
Peter Wohlleben: *The Hidden Life of Trees: What They Feel, How They Communicate* (2015).

Web & Online Sources
American Academy of Arts & Sciences – *The Universe Is Stranger Than We Thought*:
   https://www.amacad.org/news/universe-stranger-we-thought
Arts of Thought – Carl Jung, Synchronicity:
   https://artsofthought.com/2020/05/30/carl-jung-synchronicity/
Britannica – Human Body:
   https://www.britannica.com/science/human-body
Britannica – Information Theory / Physiology:
   https://www.britannica.com/science/information-theory/Physiology
David Hamilton – Is There Science on Reiki?:
   https://drdavidhamilton.com/is-there-science-on-reiki/
Dr Gabor Maté – Real Reason Women Smokers at Greater Risk:
   https://drgabormate.com/real-reason-women-smokers-great-er-risk/#:~:text=Women%20are%20thus%20conditioned%20to,also%20related%20to%20lung%20cancer.

Engage Group – Saying We're All Burnt Out:
https://engagegroup.co.uk/blog/news-and-events/saying-were-all-burnt-out-stops-us-helping-those-who-really-are/#:~:text=More%20than%20three%2Dquarters%20(79,with%20at%20least%20100%20employees

Greater Good Science Center – Gratitude Study PDF:
https://greatergood.berkeley.edu/pdfs/GratitudePDFs/6Emmons-BlessingsBurdens.pdf

Harvard Medical School – Half the World's Population Will Experience Mental Health Disorder:
https://hms.harvard.edu/news/half-worlds-population-will-experience-mental-health-disorder

LinkedIn – Marc Randolph on Work and Career:
https://www.linkedin.com/posts/marcrandolph_ive-worked-hard-for-my-entire-career-to-activity-7015671841243418624-SEtt/

Mesopotamia – Wikipedia:
https://en.wikipedia.org/wiki/Mesopotamia

Enki – Wikipedia:
https://en.wikipedia.org/wiki/Enki#:~:text=Enki%20(Sumerian%3A%20%F0%92%80%AD%F0%92%82%97%F0%92%86%A0)%20is,(Assyrian%20and%20Babylonian)%20mythology.

Pew Research Center – Demographics of Remarriage:
https://www.pewresearch.org/social-trends/2014/11/14/chapter-2-the-demographics-of-remarriage/

Performance Science – Sing With Us:
https://performancescience.ac.uk/singwithus/

Pim van Lommel – Near-Death Experience:
https://pimvanlommel.nl/en/near-death-experience/experience/

Psychology Today – Mental Health Benefits of Singing in a Choir:
https://www.psychologytoday.com/gb/blog/evidence-based-living/202307/the-mental-health-benefits-of-singing-in-a-choir#:~:text=A%20study%20of%20cancer%20caregivers,and%20boosted%20the%20immune%20system.

ResearchGate – The Energetic Heart: Bioelectromagnetic Interactions Within and Between People:
https://www.researchgate.net/

publication/274451622_The_Energetic_Heart_Biolectromagnetic_
Interactions_Within_and_Between_People

Scientific American – The Universe Is Not Locally Real, Nobel Prize
Proof:
https://www.scientificamerican.com/article/the-universe-is-not-lo-
cally-real-and-the-physics-nobel-prize-winners-proved-it/

ScienceDaily – Mental Practice in Training:
https://www.scirp.org/reference/referencespapers?referen-
ceid=928157#:~:text=Results%20showed%20that%20mental%20
practice,of%20this%20approach%20in%20training

ScienceDaily – Neural Processing Study (2010):
https://www.sciencedaily.com/releases/2010/07/100723161221.
htm

ScienceDaily – Sleep/Memory Study (2019):
https://www.sciencedaily.com/releases/2019/09/190930214514.
htm

Rupert Sheldrake – Animal Powers (Dogs Knowing When Owners
Return):
https://www.sheldrake.org/research/animal-powers/a-dog-that-
seems-to-know-when-his-owner-is-coming-home-videotaped-ex-
periments-and-observations#:~:text=First%2C%20the%20dog%20
could%20be,the%20absent%20person%20is%20returning.

Rupert Sheldrake – Morphic Resonance Introduction:
https://www.sheldrake.org/research/morphic-resonance/
introduction

Sites.Socsci.UCI.edu – Wishing, Money and Anthropology:
https://sites.socsci.uci.edu/~wmmaurer/courses/anthro_
money_2006/wishing.html

Thames Water Still Using Dowsing – Yahoo News:
https://uk.news.yahoo.com/thames-water-still-using-
dowsing-165511070.html?guccounter=1&guce_refer-
rer=aHR0cHM6Ly9nZW1pbmkuZ29vZ2xlLmNvbS8&guce_
referrer_sig=AQAAACr0IboQEUMztUyyYWd38Jzx4B0Ty0eEXjz-
ZoHrnILj33xUD9AsnM7gAibqprUiWnV90yDGnJ1xalf3wY-EO-
EU2ShcgbpNXPH-KPQCuAuO90AG1XImUahhnx_oUI1lG-FX-
kOE9a5yl03tu0XoqK10zoQEH-h15TQNasaeUmPyAQA

TikTok – @gettingwitchywitit Video 1:
    https://www.tiktok.com/@gettingwitchywitit/
    video/7312670356895026474?_t=8mitcStIpjE&_r=1
TikTok – @gettingwitchywitit Video 2:
    https://www.tiktok.com/@gettingwitchywitit/
    video/7326981972302040366?_t=8mit4yx5Eci&_r=1

Endnotes

1 Vivienne Crawley, *Wild Once* (Bantam Press, 2021), p.3.
2 The Pyramid Texts, first inscribed in the pyramid of Pharaoh Unas (c.2350BCE), are the earliest surviving religious writings in the world. See James P. Allen, *The Ancient Egyptian Pyramid Texts* (Society of Biblical Literature, 2005).
3 The Hermetic writers defined magic more precisely as 'the operation of the mind and will upon nature.' Hermes Trismegistus, *Asclepius* (Corpus Hermeticum), c.2nd–3rd century CE. See: Copenhaver, Brian P. *Hermetica: The Greek Corpus Hermeticum and the Latin Asclepius in a New English Translation* (Cambridge University Press, 1992).
4 Dion Fortune was not alone in reclaiming esoteric traditions in the early twentieth century. Other influential voices included Aleister Crowley, whose Thelemic system emphasised ritual magic and personal will; Israel Regardie, who preserved and published Golden Dawn teachings; and Arthur Edward Waite, co-creator of the Rider-Waite-Smith Tarot. Much of this wisdom had survived in men-only orders such as the Freemasons, Rosicrucians and, earlier, the Knights Templar – secretive societies that transmitted esoteric knowledge through ritual and symbolism. Fortune herself trained in the Alpha et Omega, a successor branch of the Hermetic Order of the Golden Dawn, before founding her own group in 1924: the Society of the Inner Light. Her legacy is especially significant here, as she advanced this wisdom in a climate where women were far more vulnerable to dismissal and exclusion than their male contemporaries.
5 Dion Fortune, *The Training and Work of an Initiate* (Rider & Co., 1930), p.220.
6 Dion Fortune, *Applied Magic* (Aquarian Press, first published 1962; essays written c.1920s).
7 Crocker, R. M., et al. "Stardust in the Human Body". *Astrobiology* (UCSC, 2017).

8   According to a meta-analysis published in PLoS Medicine, up to 80% of the effect of antidepressants in mild to moderate depression may be due to placebo. (Kirsch et al., 2008).

9   From research by Alain Aspect, John F. Clauser, and Anton Zeilinger, who were awarded the 2022 Nobel Prize in Physics for pioneering experiments with entangled photons, establishing the foundation for modern quantum information science.

10   https://science.nasa.gov/exoplanets/what-is-the-universe/#:~:-text=In%20short%2C%20most%20of%20the,a%20few%20hundred%20thousand%20years.

11   George Land and Beth Jarman, *Breakpoint and Beyond: Mastering the Future Today* (HarperBusiness, 1993). The book reports on their 1968 NASA creativity test and the longitudinal study with 1,600 children in a Head Start program. At age five, 98% of children tested at the "genius level" of creativity. By age ten, that dropped to 30%, and by age fifteen to 12%. Among adults, only 2% scored at that level.

12   Gosselin, P. et al. (2010). "Children's ability to distinguish between enjoyment and non-enjoyment smiles." *Infant and Child Development*, 19(3), pp.297–312.

13   https://hms.harvard.edu/news/half-worlds-population-will-experience-mental-health-disorder

14   Sharon Blackie, *If Women Rose Rooted: A Journey to Authenticity and Belonging* (September Publishing, 2016), p.14.

15   Crowley, Vivianne. *Wild Once* (Rider 2022).

16   Federici, Silvia. *Caliban and the Witch: Women, the Body and Primitive Accumulation.* (Autonomedia 2004).

17   Ehrenreich, Barbara, and Deirdre English. *Witches, Midwives, and Nurses: A History of Women Healers.* (Feminist Press 1973).

18   C.G. Jung, *Synchronicity: An Acausal Connecting Principle,* (Princeton University Press, 1973), p.44.

19   Deike Begg: *Synchronicity: The Art of Coincidence, Choice, and Unlocking Your Mind* (2010).

20   Carl Jung collaborated with Nobel Prize–winning physicist Wolfgang Pauli, whose work on quantum theory helped inspire Jung's concept of *synchronicity.* Pauli proposed that psyche and matter might arise from a shared underlying reality, what they called the *unus mundus,* or "one world." Their correspondence is collected in *Atom and Archetype: The Pauli/Jung Letters, 1932–1958* (Princeton University Press, 2001).

21   W. B. Yeats, *The Celtic Twilight: Faerie and Folklore* (1893).

22 A meta-analysis of 60 studies confirmed the effect, showing that observation itself seems to influence human perception. Rupert Sheldrake, "The Sense of Being Stared At: Experiments with Randomisation and Distance," *Journal of the Society for Psychical Research* 64 (2000), pp.224–32.

23 Wiseman, R. *The Luck Factor: The four essential principles.* (Miramax Books, 2003).

24 Brown, Derren. 2011. "*The Secret of Luck.*" *The Experiments.* Channel 4, November 4.

25 Byrne, Rhonda. *The Magic.* (Atria Books, 2012).

26 You can do this in any way that suits you, but I found myself wanting an easy way to collect and look back on all the good in my life – so I created a simple free app called With Gratitude.

27 Vivianne Crowley, *Wild Once: Awaken the Magic Within* (Cornerstone Press, 2022).

28 Harvard Business Review. "Decoding Intuition for More Effective Decision-Making" (2011), [online] Available at: https://hbr.org/2011/08/decoding-intuition-for-more-ef) [Accessed 10 Oct. 2024].

29 LeDoux, J. *The Emotional Brain: The Mysterious Underpinnings of Emotional Life.* (Simon & Schuster, 1996). In this work, LeDoux discusses how the amygdala enables rapid emotional responses, often occurring before conscious thought processes can engage.

30 Hermann Keyserling, *The Travel Diary of a Philosopher* (Harcourt, Brace & Company, 1925).

31 Henry Corbin, "Mundus Imaginalis, or the Imaginary and the Imaginal," *Spring* Journal, 1972; reprinted in *Swedenborg and Esoteric Islam* (Princeton University Press, 1995)

32 Sheldrake, R. *Dogs That Know When Their Owners are Coming Home* (Three Rivers Press, 1999).

33 Sheldrake, R. *Dogs That Know When Their Owners are Coming Home* (Three Rivers Press, 1999).

34 Brown & Sheldrake, 1998; Sheldrake, Lawlor & Turney, 1998; Sheldrake & Smart, 1997.

35 News, A. (2003). Excerpt: "The Sense of Being Stared At". [online] ABC News. Available at: https://abcnews.go.com/GMA/story?id=125298&page=1 [Accessed 10 Oct. 2024].

36 Sheldrake, R. (n.d.). "Think someone's staring at you? "Sixth sense" may be biological". [online] Rupert Sheldrake – Author and Biologist. Available at: https://

www.sheldrake.org/about-rupert-sheldrake/interviews/
think-someone-s-staring-at-you-sixth-sense-may-be-biological.

37   Erwin Schrödinger, "Discussion of Probability Relations Between
Separated Systems", in *Proceedings of the Cambridge Philosophical
Society* 31 (1935): 555–563. This paper introduced the term
Verschränkung, later translated as "entanglement".

38   Garisto, D. ,"The universe is not locally real, and the physics
nobel prize winners proved it" *Scientific American* (2024).
Available at: https://www.scientificamerican.com/article/the-uni-
verse-is-not-locally-real-and-the-physics-nobel-prize-winners-
proved-it/ (Accessed: 24 February 2025).

39   From research by Alain Aspect, John F. Clauser, and Anton
Zeilinger, who were awarded the 2022 Nobel Prize in Physics for
pioneering experiments with entangled photons, establishing the
foundation for modern quantum information science.

40   Rupert Sheldrake, *The Sense of Being Stared At: And Other Aspects
of the Extended Mind* (Hutchinson, 2003).

41   Benebell Wen, *Holistic Tarot: An Integrative Approach to Using
Tarot for Personal Growth* (North Atlantic Books, 2015).

42   Benebell Wen, *Holistic Tarot: An Integrative Approach to Using
Tarot for Personal Growth* (North Atlantic Books, 2015).

43   Lingard, L. *Divination* (2021).

44   Rippin, Peter John. *Adventures with a Pendulum.* (CreateSpace
Independent Publishing Platform, 2016).

45   Rhys Blakely, "Thames Water and Severn Trent Water Still Use
Dowsing to Detect Leaks" , (*The Times,* 2023), https://www.
thetimes.com/article/thames-water-and-severn-trent-water-still-
use-dowsing-to-detect-leaks

46   Israel Regardie, *The Tree of Life: A Study in Magic* (Rider, 1932;
repr. Weiser Books, 1972)

47   Abramson, A. "Burnout and Stress Are Everywhere. [online]
American Psychological Association". (2022). Available at:
https://www.apa.org/monitor/2022/01/special-burnout-stress.

48   Midilli, T. et al. (2015). *Holistic Nursing Practice,* 29(5),
pp.284–293.

49   Studies by Dr. Helene Langevin and others show that chronic
tension can cause fascial tissues to stiffen, restricting fluid
exchange and altering nervous system signalling. Helene M.
Langevin et al., "Fascia and the Mechanisms of Acupuncture,"
Journal of Bodywork and Movement Therapies 5, no. 2 (2001):
118–128. Trauma research further demonstrates that unresolved

stress can hold the body in a persistent sympathetic ("fight-or-flight") state, linked with systemic inflammation and disease risk: Bessel van der Kolk, *The Body Keeps the Score: Brain, Mind, and Body in the Healing of Trauma* (New York: Viking, 2014).

50 McCraty, R., Atkinson, M., Tomasino, D., & Bradley, R. T. (2009). "The coherent heart: Heart–brain interactions, psycho-physiological coherence, and the emergence of system-wide order." *Integral Review*, 5(2), pp.10–115.

51 Giese-Davis, J., et al. "Emotion Regulation, Repressive Coping, and Health in Breast Cancer Patients." *Journal of Psychosomatic Research*, 2002, 52(3), pp.145–153.

52 Schmidt, Lennart, et al. "Placebo effects improve sickness symptoms and drug efficacy during systemic inflammation." *BMC Medicine*, vol. 23, no. 1, 2025, article 292. https://doi.org/10.1186/s12916-025-04292-8

53 Kaptchuk, Ted J., et al. "Placebo Effects in the Treatment of Migraine: Trial of Rizatriptan." *Science Translational Medicine*, vol. 6, no. 218, 2014, 218ra5.

54 De la Fuente-Fernández, Rafael, et al. "Expectation and dopamine release: mechanism of the placebo effect in Parkinson's disease." *Science*, vol. 293, no. 5532, 2001, pp.1164–1166.

55 Table adapted from *The Secret Language of the Body*, Jennifer Mann and Kardan Rabin, p.269.

56 Dr Stanislav Grof is a Czech-born clinical psychiatrist and one of the founders of transpersonal psychology. Trained originally in psychoanalysis at Charles University in Prague, he became one of the leading researchers into the therapeutic use of LSD in the 1960s. After moving to the United States, he served as Chief of Psychiatric Research at the Maryland Psychiatric Research Center and later as a scholar-in-residence at the Esalen Institute in California. Over the course of studying more than 25,000 sessions, Grof observed that altered states of consciousness could access dimensions of the psyche far beyond the reach of conventional therapy, often leading to emotional and spiritual breakthroughs.

57 Holotropic Breathwork™ is now practised worldwide through certified facilitators trained by the Grof® Legacy Training and the Grof Transpersonal Training programs. You can find workshops and practitioner directories at www.holotropic.com or www.grof-legacy-training.com. Related breath modalities such as Conscious Connected Breathing and Rebirthing Breathwork

share the same principle – using cyclical, conscious breath to release stored emotion and restore the body's natural flow of energy. Each approach differs slightly in technique and philosophy, but all work towards the same outcome: rapid, integrative healing through the wisdom of breath.

58 Noetel, M., Sanders, T., Gallardo-Gómez, D., Taylor, P., Cruz, B. del P., Hoek, D. van den, Smith, J.J., Mahoney, J., Spathis, J., Moresi, M., Pagano, R., Pagano, L., Vasconcellos, R., Arnott, H., Varley, B., Parker, P., Biddle, S. and Lonsdale, C. (2024). "Effect of exercise for depression: systematic review and network meta-analysis of randomised controlled trials". *BMJ*, [online] 384(8417), p.e075847. doi:https://doi.org/10.1136/bmj-2023-075847.

59 Less than 8% of adults in England engage in daily physical activity. *The Times*, "10 Things Men and Women Need to Know About Their Health". https://www.thetimes.co.uk/article/10-things-men-and-women-need-to-know-about-their-health-advice-bsgdjxcsw

60 Philip Carr-Gomm. *Druidcraft*. (HarperThorsons, 2002).

61 Philip Carr-Gomm is a psychologist and former leader of the Order of Bards, Ovates and Druids. See *Druid Mysteries: Ancient Wisdom for the 21st Century* (Rider, 2002).

62 The Innocence Project. "Eyewitness Identification Reform". www.innocenceproject.org.

63 I first learned about *magical seduction* from Dr Kate Tomas via her website. She regularly hosts workshops in this area, and I wholeheartedly recommend signing up. Dr Tomas holds a Doctorate of Philosophy in Theology from the University of Oxford and a Master's degree in the Philosophy of Religion from the University of Kent, and she teaches philosophy, mysticism, and ritual practice. You can find her work at: www.drkatetomas.com.

64 Y. Obayashi, Shintaro Uehara, Akiko Yuasa & Yohei Otaka, "The other person's smiling amount affects one's smiling response during face-to-face conversations" *Frontiers in Behavioral Neuroscience*, Vol. 18 (2024).

65 Psychologists reached this conclusion by measuring authenticity directly and comparing it with mental health outcomes, finding that living in alignment with oneself predicts wellbeing even when income, education, and intelligence are held constant. See Wood et al., *Journal of Counseling Psychology* (2008).

66 Kosilo, M., et al. *The Neural Basis of Authenticity Recognition in Laughter* (PMC, 2021).

67 Vivienne Crowley, *Wild Once: Awaken the Magic Within* (Hachette, 2020), p.19.

68 https://pubmed.ncbi.nlm.nih.gov/2980864/

69 *The Official Witches Circle*, Instagram post.

70 American Academy of Facial Plastic and Reconstructive Surgery (2021). *Annual Survey Highlights*. Available at: https://www.aafprs.org/

71 Carl Jung, *Modern Man in Search of a Soul* (Routledge, 1933), p. 234.

72 Viola Davis, Acceptance Speech at the Film at Lincoln Center's 48th Chaplin Award Gala, New York City, April 24, 2023.

73 This is a modern paraphrase of a sentiment found in her letters, especially her Letter 368 to Stefano di Corrado Maconi (written around 1376–1378).

74 Albert Bandura, *Social Learning Theory* (Englewood Cliffs, NJ: Prentice-Hall, 1977).

75 Carl Jung, *Psychological Reflections: A New Anthology of His Writings* (Princeton University Press, 1953).

76 Marina Tsvetaeva, *Earthly Signs: Moscow Diaries, 1917–1922*, trans. Jamey Gambrell (Yale University Press, 2002).

77 Jill Purce, *The Mystic Spiral: Journey of the Soul* (Thames and Hudson, 1974).

78 Livingston, G. The Demographics of Remarriage. (2014) [online] Pew Research Center's Social & Demographic Trends Project. Available at: https://www.pewresearch.org/social-trends/2014/11/14/chapter-2-the-demographics-of-remarriage/.

79 Dion Fortune, *The Mystical Qabalah*, (Williams & Norgate, 1930).

80 Dion Fortune. *Applied Magic*. (Red Wheel/Weiser, 2000) .p.15.

81 Dion Fortune. *Applied Magic*. (Red Wheel/Weiser, 2000) .p.15.

82 Jill Purce, *The Mystic Spiral: Journey of the Soul* (Thames and Hudson, 1974).

83 Raymond A. Moody, *Life After Life: The Investigation of a Phenomenon – Survival of Bodily Death* (HarperOne, 1975).

84 Felicity Warner, interview with David Lorimer, *Imaginal Inspirations* podcast, RedCircle, episode published 2021. Available at: https://redcircle.com/shows/imaginal-inspirations/episodes/8490884a-a2f4-48c6-8406-9a01116d2d34

85 Michael Newton, *Journey of Souls: Case Studies of Life Between Lives* (1994).

86 Elisabeth Kübler-Ross, *On Life After Death* (1991).

87 Miles Richardson et al., "The Decline of Nature Words in English Literature Since 1800", *Earth* (2025).

88 World Economic Forum. (n.d.). Fewer children than ever know the names for plants and animals. [online] Available at: https://www.weforum.org/agenda/2019/09/children-are-forgetting-the-names-for-plants-and-animals/.

89 Exeter.ac.uk. Featured news – New research finds coastal living linked with better mental health – University of Exeter. (2020) [online] Available at: https://www.exeter.ac.uk/news/featured-news/title_754908_en.html [Accessed 10 Oct. 2024].

90 Seminal works by Rachel and Stephen Kaplan laid the foundation for this theory. They introduced the concept of "soft fascination", where natural elements like clouds, rustling leaves, or flowing water gently engage our attention without demanding focus, allowing our minds to recover.

91 Li Q. "Effect of forest bathing trips on human immune function". *Environ Health Prev Med*, 2010 Jan;15(1):9-17. doi: 10.1007/s12199-008-0068-3. PMID: 19568839; PMCID: PMC2793341.

92 Ulrich, R.S. "View through a window may influence recovery from surgery". (1984) *Science*, 224 (4647), pp.420–421. https://doi.org/10.1126/science.6143402.

93 Sheldrake, Merlin. *Entangled Life: How Fungi Make Our Worlds, Change Our Minds & Shape Our Futures*. (Random House, 2020).

94 Medicinal Botany. [online] Available at: https://www.fs.usda.gov/wildflowers/ethnobotany/medicinal/index.shtml.

95 If you're unsure yet which flower you want to work with, be open to any plant that attracts your attention. Maybe you see a certain plant everywhere, or you spot one that really draws you in. Approach the flower that is waving or "calling" to you. Breathe with it and make friends, introducing yourself and explaining the sort of help you are looking for and why. When communicating with the flower, ask about its medicinal powers. Listen carefully through the heart space and trust your intuition.

96 Brown glass bottles, like amber glass bottles, protect flower essences effectively by blocking UV rays that can break down the essences.

97 Sharon Blackie, *If Women Rose Rooted: A Journey to Authenticity and Belonging* (September Publishing, 2016).

98 Schjoedt, Uffe et al. "Rituals Reduce Anxiety in a Non-Western Cultural Setting". *Religion, Brain & Behavior* (2020).

99 Sender R, Fuchs S, Milo R. "Revised Estimates for the Number of Human and Bacteria Cells in the Body". (2016). PLoS Biol 14(8): e1002533. doi:10.1371/journal.pbio.1002533

100 Cain, C. (2014, June 5). "Rafael Nadal's ritual tic is really a method to find focus. For The Win". https://ftw-eu.usatoday.com/story/sports/tennis/2014/06/05/rafael-nadal-ritual-tic-pick-water-bottles/82150364007/

101 Randolph, Marc. "I've Worked Hard for My Entire Career to Keep This One Rule". *LinkedIn*, January 23, 2023. https://www.linkedin.com/posts/marcrandolph_ive-worked-hard-for-my-entire-career-to-activity-7015671841243418624-SEtt

102 Scott Cunningham, *Earth Power: Techniques of Natural Magic* (1983).

103 Leyla Zengin Aydın & Aysel Doğan, "The Effect of Guided Imagery on Postoperative Pain Management in Patients Undergoing Lower Extremity Surgical Operations: A Randomized Controlled Trial", *Orthopaedic Nursing* 42, no.2 (2023), pp.105–112.

104 Gollwitzer, Peter & Sheeran, Paschal. "Implementation Intentions and Goal Achievement: A Meta-Analysis of Effects and Processes" (2006). First publ. in: Advances in Experimental Social Psychology 38 (2006), pp.69–119. 38. 10.1016/S0065-2601(06)38002-1.

105 Lauder, Estée. *Estée: A Success Story.* (Random House, 1985).

About the author

Poppy Jamie is a writer, broadcaster, cognitive scientist and mystic. She hosted *Unwind with Poppy*, one of the UK's top spiritual wellness podcasts. She was awarded the Prime Minister's Point of Light honour for her work in mental health, is a Forbes 30 Under 30 recognised entrepreneur, and holds a degree from the LSE alongside a postgraduate degree in Psychosynthesis.

IG @poppyjamie